Cafe Fina's Cookbook

You Don't Have to be a Chef to Cook Great Food

*To Lori
Enjoy the cookbook
Best wishes
Dominic*

page 140 the Best

By Dominic Mercurio

with Sally Baho

Text and photographs copyright © 2023 by Dominic Mercurio

All rights reserved. No part of this book may be reproduced or used in any manner without the prior written permission of the copyright owner, except in the case of reprints in the context of reviews.

Library of Congress Control Number: 2023914764

ISBN: 9798396752696

Photography and design: Sally Baho, unless otherwise noted and not including the photographs from Dominic Mercurio's collection of family and personal photos.

Cover photo by Kelli Uldall.

For more information on ordering copies of this book contact Cafe Fina:

Cafe Fina
47 Fisherman's Wharf No. 1
Monterey, CA 93940
www.cafefina.com
finefood@cafefina.com

10 9 8 7 6 5 4 3 2 1

DEDICATION

This book is in loving memory of my grandparents, Santo & Santa Pisto and Salvator & Giolorma Mercurio.

It is dedicated to my mother and father, Josephine and Jean Mercurio, who taught me the importance of character, not only at our mandatory Sunday afternoon family dinners, but as they walked through life. Looking back now, I understand the importance of gathering as a family, being held accountable, and having felt unconditional love around the dinner table.

To my two children, Kathryn Donangelo and Dominic J. Mercurio, who I am very proud of and in whom I have instilled the integrity that my parents instilled in me.

Kathryn continues my passion for food in her amazing food blog and she continues the tradition of family dinners. My son-in-law, Matthew Donangelo, is a great husband and together with Kathryn has two lovely daughters, Gianna and Mia.

The career Dominic has chosen—to protect and serve—is a difficult one, but admirable and very important. Your hard work and integrity are paying off.

Matt, Kathryn, Gianna, and Mia Donangelo

Dominic with his niece, Gianna

CONTENTS

	Family Photos	iix
	Acknowledgments	xvii
	Foreword	xix
	Introduction	xxi
	John Madden Tribute	xxv
1	Appetizers & Sides	1
2	Soups, Stews, & Salads	31
3	Sauces & Dressings	49
4	Pasta	63
5	Seafood	91
6	Other Good Stuff	111
7	Dessert & Drinks	133
	Index	152

June 28, 1989 – opening night of Cafe Fina

FAMILY PHOTOS

My mom, Josephine Mercurio, as a little girl (top left). My maternal grandparents and relatives in Furci Siculo (top right). My dad, Jean Mercurio, and cousin, Vince Crivello, fishing tuna in South America (bottom left). My grandfather, Uncle John, grandmother, mother, and Aunt Betty at a train station in Italy (bottom right).

My mom's high school graduation photo with her best friends, (left to right) Genevieve, Joanne, Josephine, and Mary (top left). The same friends, Genevieve, Mom, and Joanne, in 2022 at Cafe Fina (top right). Dad fishing in Alaska (bottom left). The Monterey Wharf with its original wood planks before it was paved (bottom right, photo courtesy of the Pat Hathaway Collection).

Dad fishing in South America (top left). Dad at Uncle John's house getting ready for a feast (top right). Dad sitting on fishing nets on a boat (bottom left). Grandparents and relatives in Pacific Grove, me as a child (bottom right).

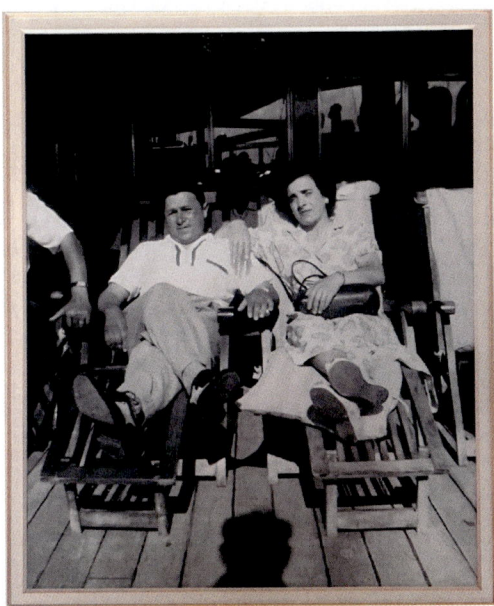

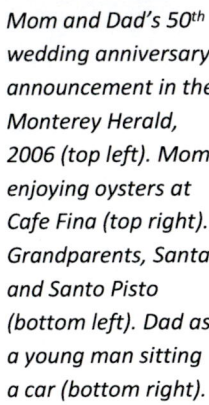

Mom and Dad's 50th wedding anniversary announcement in the Monterey Herald, 2006 (top left). Mom enjoying oysters at Cafe Fina (top right). Grandparents, Santa and Santo Pisto (bottom left). Dad as a young man sitting a car (bottom right).

My grandparents at a picnic at the park (top left). Dad with fresh-caught salmon (top right). Family at Veteran's Park in Monterey (bottom left). Dad mending nets with my Uncle Pierre (bottom right).

My daughter, Kathryn, and me at the KCBS BBQ for John Madden (left; photo by Elaine Hesser). My son, Dominic, and, his dog, Tulle, and me duck hunting (bottom right). My mom and dad (bottom left).

A typical Sunday meal at my aunt and uncle's home on Spaghetti Hill in Monterey, around 1950.

My maternal grandparents, Santo and Santa Pisto.

ACKNOWLEDGMENTS

To the late John Madden, who had a saying that I live by, "If you don't want to read about it in the paper, don't do it."

And my dear friend, Carl Panattoni, who once told me when I needed some advice, "always take the high road."

Both of these gentlemen opened doors for me that changed my life, and I'm eternally grateful.

Carl Panattoni and me duck hunting

To Sally Baho,

Timing is everything.
Your talents are amazing.
Thank you for all your hard work and patience with me.
Your passion for food is what made this friendship work.
I could not have done this without you.
You are amazing.

-Dominic

I have learned so much working with Dominic—from how to cook a whole octopus, to the difference between marinara and pizza sauce—but the most important thing I've learned from Dominic is the importance of character. Dominic is the most honest man I know, and he has integrity. He may not tell you what you want to hear, but he will tell you what you need to hear. And if he says he is going to do something, you can put your life on it. Thank you for this opportunity, Dominic.

-Sally Baho

Photo courtesy of Doug Steakley (opposite).

Lance Barrow, John Madden, and me in front of Cafe Fina.

FOREWORD

I first came to the Monterey Peninsula in the late 1970s when I was still in college at Abilene Christian University and working for Pat Summerall at CBS Sports. We were traveling to cover the Bing Crosby Pebble Beach Pro-Am, which is known today as the AT&T Pebble Beach Pro-Am.

One of my favorite things to do on the road is to find great restaurants. The restaurants on the Monterey Peninsula are some of the best in the world and very diverse; you could eat a different cuisine every night. During my time with Pat, he was paired with the legendary coach John Madden to cover the NFL on CBS. John would eventually become like a second father to me. One thing that John and I had in common was our love of food and enjoying meals together. Starting in the late 1990s, Davis Love III, Mike Hulbert, Joey Sindelar—all successful PGA Tour players at that time—along with John and I, started a tradition of having dinner Monday night the week of the Pebble Beach Pro-Am.

John had taken many trips to the Monterey Peninsula and had met Dominic Mercurio who owned Cafe Fina on the Monterey Wharf. On John's recommendation—we didn't really have an option—our group tried Cafe Fina. That was where my friendship with Dominic was born. Dominic's family were known as restaurateurs and fishermen and Cafe Fina serves a mix of their fresh seafood, as well as Italian dishes. My first memory of Cafe Fina was sitting upstairs against the window overlooking the Monterey Bay. We sat down, and before we could even think about a menu, Dominic began to bring us food. One of the first things we had...and that I was reluctant to try, was his smoked salmon pizza (I have been eating it ever since). We also had fried calamari and locally grown whole steamed artichokes, followed by pasta with the best meatballs I have ever had. After eating for over an hour, Dominic handed us menus. I thought the meal was over, but I soon learned that that's how meals go at Cafe Fina. That night changed our tradition from Monday night dinners to Monday night dinners at Cafe Fina. Over time, as people heard of these dinners, our party grew to upwards of 30 people. Every time we ate at Cafe Fina with John he would always ask when the next dish was coming; he would call Dominic over and jokingly ask him if we were at a museum or were we going to eat at all that night.

Some of my fondest memories of Pebble Beach are dinners at Cafe Fina. Dominic has become more than a friend; he has become part of my family and he has always treated them in the same regard. No trip to Monterey is complete without a meal at Cafe Fina. I am looking forward to Dominic's cookbook and happy that he is sharing with the world some of the dishes he has shared with me over the years. This cookbook is his way of inviting you to become part of the Cafe Fina family.

Lance Barrow, producer, CBS Sports

INTRODUCTION

I learned how to cook by watching my mom and by working with her brother—my Uncle John—first at the Captain's Gig on the Wharf and then at his restaurant, the Whaling Station, when he opened it in 1972. My mother was born in New York to Sicilian parents. When she was 8 years old, they moved to Monterey and my maternal grandparents opened a tailor shop downtown. Not only were they businessowners, but they did all the tailoring for the Army officers at Fort Ord and the Defense Language Institute. My mother was the oldest of the three children, so naturally, she learned to cook at age 12 so she could care for her younger siblings, my Aunt Elizabeth (Betty) and Uncle John. "I saw my mother do it, and then I improvised, I loved cooking," my mom says. "Cooking makes me happiest even though nowadays I have to sit down to do the peeling, but I still love it." My Sicilian father came from North Africa because he followed the fish; he had been fishing off the coast of Algeria when he heard about the sardines in the Monterey Bay and that's how my parents met. I grew up fishing with my dad and when I was 13 my father took me on one of his fishing trips to Alaska and I have been hooked since.

Cooking starts with good ingredients. My mom, even though she's 87 years old, refuses to order her groceries online or have someone shop for her; she has to go to the store herself and see and touch the produce. "I have to see what's fresh, and I buy that," she says. The other thing about cooking that my mom taught me is that you have to care about what you're cooking, you have to put your love in it. My father used to tell my mother, "If you don't put your love in your food, it doesn't come out good." So, if you don't like to cook, your food won't turn out well, it's that simple. My mom says, "You have to love what you're doing. If you don't like it, don't do it, you're wasting your time. Sometimes my husband would tell me, 'You didn't put any love in this tonight.' He could tell if I was in a bad mood by how my food turned out." But that didn't happen very often.

As a kid, my mom would sit me on the counter while she cooked. She chopped garlic for just about everything, but my favorite was watching her make Italian salad dressing. She would let me help her chop the garlic and it was supposed to be very fine, so she would tell me to keep going if it wasn't to her liking. We would put that in a coffee mug and add olive oil and vinegar. Then a bay leaf—that she had dried herself—and a bit of ketchup, oregano, salt, pepper, and some thyme. She stirred it up with a fork and that's what we had on our salads almost every day. You'll see a variation of this…

One of my mom's favorite family traditions around food is the Feast of Seven Fishes for Christmas Eve. "I like Christmas Eve more than Christmas Day because we have all the fish dishes: clams, octopus, shrimp, squid, mussels, crab, and oysters," she says. Some other Italian families just do crab and artichokes, but my father was a fisherman and having all the connections we do in Monterey, we are always able to get fresh fish. You'll see that many of the recipes in this book involve seafood because I'm a fisherman and I'm Sicilian.

I named my restaurant Cafe Fina after my mother, Josephina. I bought the restaurant Geno's from the patriarch of the Genovese family, renamed it Cafe Fina, and opened it in 1989. It has been home to me ever since. I have poured my heart and soul into Cafe Fina, and this cookbook is a way to capture my mom's recipes, and everything that Cafe Fina has become over the years. I want to put her recipes down on paper so future generations can enjoy a taste of my mother's cooking, love, and share it with their friends and families, too. The handwritten recipes separating the chapters are her handwriting, from her recipe book, "Nana's Favorite Recipes" that she uses to this day. You don't have to be a professionally trained chef to make good food, but you do have to love what you're doing.

Dominic Mercurio, Owner of Cafe Fina

Renovating the restaurant before opening Cafe Fina, 1989.

A dinner with Julia Child, friends, and family at Domenico's on the Wharf. In 1981 my Uncle John and I opened Domenico's on the Wharf; I sold my share in it to open Cafe Fina in the late 80s. Several years later my brother, Sam, and I purchased it back and I remain part owner.

IN LOVING MEMORY OF JOHN MADDEN
1936-2021

My friendship with John was built on a mutual love for food, poker, and golf...and in that order.

It started one Sunday about 30 years ago (1993); I was working at the restaurant when a mountain of a man walked up with his wife. They looked at the menu and walked away, but came back, so I asked them what they were looking for. The man was polite and said, "I'm just looking for some good clam chowder." I pointed to a table in the corner and told them, "Go sit down. I'll bring you the chowder. If you don't like it, don't pay, and don't come back."

The man ended up being John Madden, the famous football coach. He and his wife came back the next seven Sundays. I was nervous at first. John was big, as big in personality as he was in stature. And he had a voice that just bellowed out. On one of those Sundays, he asked if I liked to play cards. "Yeah," I said, "I like to play cards." "You got guys?" he asked. "Yeah, I got guys," I said. "Okay, I got some guys, too. Why don't we get a poker game going?" he asked, eagerly.

I thought to myself, "I'm not playing poker with John Madden. I don't have that kind of money." I was only in my third year at Cafe Fina. Maybe he could sense my hesitation, so he said, "$40 buy-in." He smiled, "We're just doing it for fun." "All right, I'll give it a shot. I got nothing to lose. Forty bucks, maybe 80 if I buy in twice." I didn't want him to think I couldn't afford to play a couple rounds of poker. That turned into a 28-year game and a lifelong friendship.

When you started the day out with John, you never knew where you were going to end up. One day we played golf in the afternoon at Carmel Valley Ranch and ended up coming down to Cafe Fina for dinner and had a three-hour dinner, BSing and as John would say, it was a "hang." It was always a 2–3-hour dinner with John.

John's tribute table has been at Cafe Fina as a fun gesture for over 10 years. When John and Ted Hendricks—a fellow Pro Football Hall of Famer—came into the restaurant, they drew that play on the chalk board and we've left it there ever since (opposite).

One time, we walked off the Wharf at 9:00 or 9:30 at night and saw the squid boats going out at Wharf No. 2. I recognized one of the boats as my brother's and said, "Let's go take a look, I think that's where Sam's boat's at."

We drove over and my brother said, "Why don't you guys come out, I'll bring you in when you want." The next thing we knew, my brother was in a screaming match with another captain whose boat was too close to his nets. It ended up being a territorial war. It was 4 o'clock in the morning when we finally came back in. John didn't mind one bit, he loved the adventure.

On a trip I had planned with John to go watch the Green Bay Packers play, I told John I wanted to learn how to make bratwurst the right way. "I'll see what I can do. I can't guarantee it. Can't you just come and enjoy the game and relax?" he said.

No, not really, I couldn't. So, we met at the hotel in Green Bay, and we drove to the stadium in the Madden cruiser. The fans were going wild as John pulled into the stadium. As we were pulling into the players' parking lot, I noticed a giant van that had Johnsonville on the side of it. "What's that?" I asked John.

"You wanted to learn how to cook brats. So, I called the president of Johnsonville. You're going to learn how to cook brats." That day I ended up making about 200 brats for the entire NBC crew right there in Lambeau Field. The right way.

Another time, it was a busy Saturday at the restaurant and John called me up and said "Why don't we play a few holes of golf?" He said it's only 3 o'clock, it's between lunch and dinner, he called it the whiskey loop, holes 1, 2, 3, 17 and 18 at MPCC. I told him I couldn't, and he said, "That's bullshit, I just told my agent I couldn't go to the ESPEs because I had something to do. Of course you can leave the restaurant for two hours."

You had no choice with John. This was probably one of the only times we didn't have a bet. We always bet on golf and it was usually for five or 10 bucks. That day I was hitting the ball pretty good and as we were walking off the second green I said to John, "If we're ever going to get a hole-in-one it's going to be on this next hole."

He said, "If I were you I would concentrate on just getting it on the green and don't worry about the hole-in-one." We laughed and got back to playing and on the next swing, I hit a hole-in-one. We looked at each other in shock. Expletives were flying and we started walking towards the hole.

I told John that I thought we needed to have two witnesses plus myself to make it a legitimate hole-in-one and John stood up tall and said, "What are they going to call me, a liar?"

KCBS BBQ

The marshal happened to drive by in a golf cart and John was ecstatic. He was more excited than I was. The marshal told us the hole-in-one protocol, and, as it turned out, you have to play at least 14 holes and you can average the last four. We looked at each other and I said, "John, I've got to get back to work, I'm not supposed to be here." John said, "I'm not supposed to be here, either." But we had to play the nine more holes to make it count, so we did.

The marshal waved everyone out of the way for us, letting us play so we could finish quickly and I could get back to work. We ended up playing the full 18 holes because I was playing so well—I almost hit a second hole-in-one—and you had no choice with John.

When we got back to the clubhouse, John told everyone, "Dom got a hole-in-one!" He was so excited. As protocol has it, if you hit a hole-in-one, you have to buy everyone at the clubhouse a drink, so John told the waiter, "Hey, he hit a hole-in-one." The waiter responded quietly, "Great, we'll put him in the computer with his photo and everyone will get a drink on the house."

John cut him off, saying, "No, he's buying everyone a drink with actual money." And so I did.

John loved life and wouldn't take no for an answer. He always knew how to have a good time.

My brother, Sam Mercurio (top left) and me (bottom left) at the KCBS BBQ at John's Studio in Pleasanton. At the promotion party for the release of John's "Ultimate Tailgate Cookbook," featured on Good Morning America, *at Tavern on the Green in New York City, Sandy Montag, John's agent (center right) and John's bus drivers, Willie and Joe, with me (bottom right).*

David DiPietro and George Leonard who were part of the success of Pro Football Hall of Fame induction party for John in Canton, OH (top left). The Cafe Fina Crew at the Pro Football Hall of Fame induction (top right). A pig on a spit prepared by Danny Fialho (bottom left). John and I making an ad for Ragu (bottom right).

John having the final touches done on his bust for the Pro Football Hall of Fame; we were going to the Hall of Fame induction and stopped in Utah for that (top). Me in the booth at a football game with John (bottom).

Nanna's Favorite Recipes

Lentil Soup

Rinse 1 lb lentils and put in pot with 5 qts water, add 1 cup each of onion, carrots, celery, 2 Beef Bouillon cubes, 1 small can Tomato Sauce, let simmer about 50 min — add pasta, 2 cup chopped Swiss chard, (Pesto cube) — Boil an the 10 min — Serve with Italian Cheese.

Tortellini Soup

Boil 1 pt Tortellini until tender, drain and add to 1 large can Swanson Chicken Broth, add 1 cup green peas — 1 C. Green Onion, add 3 cups chopped lecalone — add 2 beaten eggs with ½ C. grating cheese — close fire. Remove from heat.

Pasta w/ Peas

Sauté 1 onion w/ 1 clove garlic in

CHAPTER 1

Appetizers & Sides

Octopus Salad
Loaded Sautéed Spinach
Whole Roasted Cauliflower
How to Cook Artichokes
Cream of Swiss Chard
Pan-fried Sardines
Fresh BBQ'd Sardines
Cauliflower Mashed Potatoes
Roasted Garlic
Braised Red Cabbage
Crabcakes
Steamed Clams
Bruschetta
Sautéed Mussels
Orzo Pasta
Rustic Olive Bread
Italian Sausage & Spinach Egg Bites
Italian-Style Roasted Peppers
Grilled Octopus
Seasoned Italian Breadcrumbs
Seasoned Cracker Meal
Crostini

Octopus Salad

Serves 6-8

Octopus salad was normally on our dinner table for the holidays, and we loved it because it was a special treat.

1 3–5-pound frozen octopus, from your local fishmonger, in Monterey that's Monterey Fish Co. on Wharf No. 2
2 bay leaves
Juice of 1 ½ lemons, separated
¼ cup red wine vinegar
½ cup olive oil
3-4 cloves finely chopped fresh garlic
¼ cup fresh chopped Italian parsley
Dash of Tabasco sauce
½ cup diced celery
Salt and pepper to taste

In a large pot of salted cold water, add the bay leaves, and both the juice and the squeezed lemon. Add frozen octopus to cold water. Turn the burner on high, when the water comes to a boil, lower heat to a simmer, half cover with the lid, and let simmer for 45 minutes.

Remove the pot from the heat and let sit—in the water—for 30-45 minutes.

Remove octopus from water and cut into bite-size pieces, ½-¾ inch. It's easiest to cut each tentacle off and coin-cut those, and then the center and the head, too.

In a small bowl, make the dressing: add the rest of the lemon juice, the red wine vinegar, olive oil, garlic, fresh parsley, Tabasco sauce, celery, and salt and pepper to taste. Mix well.

In a large bowl, add the octopus and dressing. Mix well and let sit for a few hours in the refrigerator, although it's best to let sit overnight. If you do let it sit overnight, remove from refrigerator one hour before serving.

Serve with bread.

Loaded Sautéed Spinach

Serves 4-6

From the DiPietro Family in Canton, Ohio.

In 2006, John Madden asked me to cook for his Pro Football Hall of Fame Induction party, and during the process, he and I went cross country to scope out the place where we would have the party. The owners of the facility, the Dipietro family, cooked some dishes for us, and this is one that stood out as a great side.

1 lb. chopped frozen spinach, thawed and drained well
2-3 tbsp. olive oil
1 clove chopped garlic
1 baked potato, crushed or chopped with skin
¼ cup chopped, cooked bacon
½ can cannellini beans, strained
Juice from half a lemon
Salt and pepper to taste

Squeeze the spinach to remove excess moisture.

Heat olive oil in a frying pan. Add the garlic and sauté until slightly cooked but not brown. Add beans, spinach, potato, and bacon, and sauté until piping hot. Squeeze lemon juice over the dish, add salt and pepper to taste, and serve hot.

Whole Roasted Cauliflower

Serves 2-4

1 head cauliflower
1 qt. chicken stock
Tony Chachere's Creole seasoning
¼ cup sliced, lightly toasted almonds
2 anchovy filets
1 tbsp. salted butter, melted
1 clove garlic
¼ cup olive oil
¼ cup chopped Italian parsley
Dash smoked paprika
Salt and pepper to taste

Mix all ingredients, except cauliflower, chicken stock, and Tony's, in a food processor to make a sauce.

Place cauliflower face down in a stockpot and add chicken stock; if not fully covered by the stock, top it off with water. Add a few dashes of Tony's and bring to a boil. Reduce heat and let simmer for 15-20 minutes, then turn the cauliflower over and continue simmering until a fork enters the base easily, but don't overcook it. Remove cauliflower from the stock, place on a baking sheet and broil until the top is browned. While the cauliflower is in the oven, heat the prepared sauce.

Remove the cauliflower from the oven and, keeping it whole, drizzle with the warmed sauce.

How to Cook Artichokes

Serves 8-10

When my Uncle John opened the Whaling Station in the early 70s, it started out as a hippie food place and evolved into fine dining. He made a deal with the artichoke farmers in Castroville that every person who sat down was given an artichoke. When I was working there, I worked in the kitchen. I made two giant pots of artichokes every single day. To this day, I love this recipe and still use the same method for preparation and serving.

4 large artichokes, stems cut off
1 lemon, cut in half
1 tbsp. pickling spice
1 bay leaf
A few whole black peppers, but not ground pepper—it will look like dirt in the artichoke leaves
1 heaping tbsp. granulated garlic
1 tbsp. salt
Caper Vinaigrette for serving, see page 53

Place artichokes in a pot and cover with salted water. Squeeze the lemon and add the juice and squeezed lemon to the pot. Add the rest of the ingredients and place a weight, like a plate or pie pan, to keep the artichokes unde water. Cover the pot with foil and the lid. Turn on high heat and leave for 30-45 minutes. To check, remove an artichoke with tongs, get a fork and poke it in the stem end. You will know it's done when the fork goes in easily. Cook longer if necessary.

Remove from water and let cool or refrigerate.

To serve, open the artichoke up, like a flower, gently pressing down on the center while rotating the artichoke until the whole thing is opened and flat. Remove the purple leaves and the fuzzy part. Add a dab of mayonnaise to the center and with a spoon make a crater in mayonnaise and add a few tablespoons of the Caper Vinaigrette.

Cream of Swiss Chard

Serves 2-4

1 bunch fresh, or 10 oz. frozen, Swiss chard
½ cup diced yellow onion
1 stalk of celery, diced
2 tbsp. butter
½ cup strong chicken stock
Couple dashes ground nutmeg
Pepper to taste
½ cup whole milk or heavy cream
Olive oil for cooking

Sauté the onion and celery in olive oil and the 2 tbsp. of butter in a heavy-bottomed sauce pot until they are soft.

In a separate pan, blanch the Swiss chard in salted water. When cooked, drain in a colander. Press as much of the excess water out as possible.

Add the Swiss chard to the pan with the onion and celery. Then add chicken stock, a couple dashes of nutmeg, the cream or milk, and pepper. Let ingredients cook until chard is tender and has absorbed most of the sauce. Serve as is.

Pan-fried Sardines

Serves 6-8

2-3 lbs. fileted sardines
2-3 cups white wine vinegar
Flour for breading
3-4 eggs, beaten
2 cups Seasoned Italian Breadcrumbs, see page 29
Olive oil for cooking
Lemon wedges, for serving, optional
Salmoriglio sauce, for serving, see page 56

When fileting sardines, remove as many belly bones as possible. Rinse filets well with fresh water. Marinate the sardines in the vinegar for 20-25 minutes max.

Remove filets from vinegar and pat dry. Coat filets first in flour, then the beaten eggs, and lastly in the breadcrumbs. In a large skillet, cook the sardines in ¼ inch olive oil. Fry over medium heat until both sides are golden brown. (A cast iron skillet works really well for this.) Season with salt and pepper while cooking.

Serve with fresh-squeezed lemon or Salmoriglio Sauce.

My dad, Jean Mercurio, in front of the sardine fisherman's statue on Monterey Fisherman's Wharf

Fresh BBQ'd Sardines

Serves 6-8

The fish that made Monterey famous.

2-3 lbs. fresh sardines, heads and insides discarded, rinsed well, and patted dry
Sea salt
Fresh ground black pepper
Ground cumin
Green onions, optional
Salmoriglio Sauce, see page 56

Sprinkle both sides of the sardines with sea salt, black pepper, and cumin. Let sit 20-30 minutes in the refrigerator.

Roast on an open fire for about 10 minutes or until well done. Must be cooked all the way, because sardines are very oily and can be very strong tasting if undercooked.

You can grill the green onions alongside the sardines for a great accompaniment.

Serve with Salmoriglio Sauce.

Cauliflower Mashed Potatoes

Serves 6-8

4 Russet potatoes, boiled until a knife slides in with little effort, and peeled
1 head of cauliflower
1 or 2 anchovy filets
3-4 cloves of Roasted Garlic, see page 12
¼ parmesan cheese
½ cube salted butter
¼ cup freshly chopped Italian parsley
Salt and pepper to taste

Quarter the cauliflower and boil it. You can boil it in the same water that you used for the potatoes. Remove the cauliflower from water and drain well. Sauté cauliflower in olive oil with the anchovies and garlic until the cauliflower is soft.

Place all ingredients in a mixing bowl and mix with a whisk, potato masher, or electric hand mixer. Add parmesan cheese, butter, parsley, and salt and pepper. Mix well and serve hot.

Roasted Garlic

Serves 4-6

We are just 40 miles south of the Garlic Capital of the World. I love garlic and we use garlic in many of our dishes. This appetizer is always a winner.

4 heads of super colossal garlic*
Olive oil
Salt and pepper
Crostini, see page 29
Goat cheese
Kalamata olives

Preheat oven to 375°F.

Cut the top third off each head of garlic (from the side opposite the root). Place garlic heads in a pot of salted water and boil for 30 minutes. Remove from water, place in a small roasting pan with plenty of olive oil—on top of garlic, around it, don't be stingy. Season the ends with salt and pepper.

Roast for 15 minutes, cut side up, in preheated oven. Then turn over and cook for another 15-20 minutes, cut side down, until the garlic is caramelized on the cut side.

Remove with a spatula, because the garlic cloves will stick to the pan. Let cool slightly, serve cut side up, warm.

You can make ahead and reheat for serving.

Serve with 5-6 Crostinis per head of garlic, with goat cheese and kalamata olives on the side.

Braised Red Cabbage

Serves 4-6

¼ cup olive oil
1 head red cabbage, shredded
½ cup brown sugar
Pinch of whole fennel seeds
Pinch of whole anise seeds
½ cup sherry wine vinegar

In a frying pan, heat the olive oil and add all the ingredients. Sauté over medium-low heat until cabbage is soft, at least 15 minutes or more.

Serve as a side. Goes great with fish.

Crabcakes

Serves 4-6

1 lb. crab meat, fresh is best but canned will do
1 egg, beaten
2 tbsp. melted butter
¼ cup diced Italian parsley
¼ cup diced red bell pepper
1 tsp. finely chopped shallots
1 pinch dried thyme
½ cup seasoned breadcrumbs
¼ cup heavy cream
Couple dashes Tony Chachere's Creole seasoning
Panko for coating
Oil for frying
Creole mayonnaise, for serving, see page 56

In a large mixing bowl, gently mix all ingredients well by hand. Using an ice cream scoop or a tablespoon, make golf ball size patties and flatten to form. Coat with panko on both sides and pack squeeze them delicately with your hands to pack them. Deep frying is best, but pan frying will do. Cook until golden brown. If deep frying, keep oil at 350°F. Otherwise pan fry over medium heat. Either way, you want them to be golden brown.

You can prepare the patties the day before or you can bread them and freeze them for a couple weeks. If you freeze them, rebread them once defrosted and before frying.

Serve immediately with Creole mayo.

Steamed Clams

Serves 2-4

Olive oil for cooking
½ tsp. freshly chopped garlic
1 ½ lbs. whole littleneck, cherrystone, or Manila clams, rinsed in fresh water
2 tbsp. white wine
½ cup clam juice
½ tsp. freshly chopped Italian parsley
6 cherry tomatoes, cut in half
½ stick salted butter
¼ cup water, if clams are salty

Cover bottom of sauté pan with olive oil. Add garlic and brown. Add clams, white wine, clam juice, parsley, cherry tomatoes, and water; let cook for 10 minutes. Add butter, if needed. You'll want to taste the sauce for saltiness; if it's too salty, add more water.

Bruschetta

Serves 2-4

We always serve this at the restaurant during the summer because of the abundance of vine-ripened tomatoes that I grow. It's a game changer when you use homegrown ripe tomatoes.

2 cups finely diced ripe tomatoes
1 ½ tsp. fresh garlic, chopped finely
¼ cup chopped fresh basil
½ cup extra virgin olive oil
Pinch of dried oregano
2 tbsp. balsamic vinegar
Salt and pepper
Crostini, see page 29
Whole garlic cloves for rubbing crostini

Mix all ingredients except crostini and whole garlic cloves in a bowl and let stand for at least two hours.

When ready to serve, rub crostini with garlic cloves and completely cover crostini with the tomato mix.

Serve immediately.

Sautéed Mussels

Serves 2

This is one of the most popular appetizers served at Cafe Fina.

Olive oil for cooking
4 tbsp. butter
½ tbsp. chopped garlic
12 whole black mussels
2 oz. clam juice
4 oz. marinara sauce, see page 50
1 pinch black pepper
1 oz. dry white wine
½ tbsp. chili sauce, like sriracha
Fresh basil, for garnish
Crusty Italian bread, for serving

In a sauté pan, heat olive oil and butter until butter melts, then add garlic. Let garlic brown a little then add the mussels and the remaining ingredients. Cover and stir occasionally until all mussels are opened. After 5 minutes, discard any mussels that have not opened.

Garnish with fresh finely chopped fresh basil and serve with crusty Italian bread.

Orzo Pasta

Serves 2-4

We've been using this recipe for 30+ years as a side at Cafe Fina.

1 cup orzo pasta
½ stick of butter, divided in two
¼ cup green onions, finely chopped
½ cup tomato, finely diced
¼ cup black olives, finely diced
½ cup (or more) chicken stock
Salt and pepper, to taste

Boil orzo pasta in salted water until tender (follow cooking instructions on package), and drain. Place in mixing bowl and set aside. Add half the butter to the pasta and stir to melt, which will prevent pasta from sticking.

In a large pan, melt the other half of the butter, add chopped green onions, tomato, and black olives. Cook ingredients until softened. Add chicken stock. Once heated add pasta back to the pan, stirring constantly over medium-high heat (the pasta will absorb the stock). Add salt and pepper to taste. If you prefer the pasta with a little sauce add a little more chicken stock.

Serve immediately. This reheats very well; you may have to use a little chicken stock to bring it back.

Rustic Olive Bread

Makes one loaf of bread

Recipe and photo by Kathryn Donangelo.

2 tsp. instant yeast
2 ¾ cups all-purpose flour
1 cup lukewarm water (around 100-110°F)
½ tsp. salt
½ tsp. garlic powder
3 tsp. olive oil
1 cup pitted and chopped kalamata olives; make sure they are drained

Combine the first six ingredients in the bowl of a stand mixer. By hand, use a spatula to roughly combine the ingredients. Let rest for 15 minutes to activate the yeast.

Fold in the olives. Attach the dough hook and knead on medium for 5 minutes. Sprinkle in a bit more flour as needed if the dough won't release from the sides of the bowl.

Transfer the kneaded dough to an oiled bowl, cover, and allow to rise for 60 minutes in a warm place.

Punch the dough down, then transfer to a parchment-lined baking sheet. Use your hands to shape it into a loaf. Allow to rise for another 60 minutes. While dough is rising, preheat oven to 400°F.

Place a baking sheet on the bottom rack. Dust the loaf with flour and use a serrated knife to make 3-5 shallow cuts across the top. Place it on another baking sheet.

Place the baking sheet containing the dough on the middle rack of the preheated oven. Toss a half cup of water onto the hot baking sheet on the bottom rack and close the door. Bake for 30 minutes.

Let cool completely on a wire rack before slicing.

Italian Sausage & Spinach Egg Bites

Serves 6-8

Recipe and photo by Kathryn Donangelo.

My daughter, Kathryn, started helping me in the kitchen when she was very young. When she was about 10 or 12, I told her that we were going to make raviolis together. So, I sent her mom and little Dom out of the house for two hours and we made veal and mushroom raviolis from scratch, including the sauce, from start to finish. That was her first full start-to-finish cooking experience. When her mom and brother came back, we served them the meal and it was absolutely delicious. Kathryn has been cooking great food ever since.

10-16 ounces Italian sausage (usually 4-6 links with casings removed; cooked and crumbled)
1 tsp. olive oil
1 8 oz. bag fresh spinach
8 whole eggs
3 tbsp. milk
2 tbsp. green onions, chopped
Pinch of salt and pepper

Preheat oven to 375° F.

Cook your sausage in a frying pan on medium-high heat until it's completely cooked through. Drain, then transfer to a dish lined with paper towels to absorb the excess grease.

Sauté spinach in a frying pan with the olive oil for a few minutes (it will wilt quickly). Once cooked, drain the spinach and set aside.

In a large bowl, whisk together the eggs and milk until incorporated. Add the sausage, spinach, green onions, salt and pepper, and mix together.

Grease a muffin pan with nonstick cooking spray. Carefully fill each muffin cup about ¾ of the way full with the egg mixture. Bake for 18-20 minutes until fluffy. Once the bites are baked, let them cool for a few minutes. Store in an airtight container for up to a week, but I bet you they won't last that long though.

Italian-Style Roasted Peppers

Serves 4-6

Recipe and photo by Kathryn Donangelo.

6 red, yellow, or orange bell peppers, or a combination
¼ cup olive oil
½ tsp. salt
¼ tsp. black pepper
1 tbsp. capers
1 tbsp. red wine vinegar
1 clove garlic, finely chopped
Optional, red chili flakes

Preheat oven to 400° F.

Line a baking sheet with foil and grease with cooking spray or olive oil.

Wash and dry your bell peppers and place them on their sides on the baking dish. Sprinkle a pinch of salt on top and bake for 50-60 minutes, flipping the peppers halfway through cooking.

Once the bell peppers are done, they will be extremely hot. Allow them to cool for 20-30 minutes. Placing them in a paper bag to cool will make it easier to remove the skin, if you prefer them skinless.

When the peppers are cooled, remove the stems and charred skins. Cut the peppers in half, discard stems, remove the seeds, cut peppers into strips and place the strips into a bowl.

Add the remaining ingredients to the bowl and stir to combine. You can serve immediately or let sit in the refrigerator to let the flavors fuse together.

Grilled Octopus

Serves 6-10

This dish is a showstopper! When it's on the menu we can't keep it stocked enough.

1 frozen 3-5 lb. octopus from your local fishmonger, in Monterey that's Monterey Fish Co. on Wharf No. 2
1-2 bay leaves
1 lemon, juiced

For the dressing:
½ cup good extra virgin olive oil
1 tsp. chopped garlic
Zest of one lemon
Juice of one lemon
Pinch of dried rosemary
Pinch of dried thyme
Salt and pepper to taste

For the balsamic reduction:
2 cups balsamic vinegar

A large handful of bitter greens, such as red Swiss chard, beet greens, or arugula, for serving
Lemon wedges, for serving

For the dressing, mix all ingredients and let sit for at least one hour.

In a large pot of salted cold water, add a couple bay leaves, the juice of one lemon and the squeezed lemon. Add frozen octopus to cold water. Turn the burner on high. And when the water comes to a boil, lower heat to a simmer, half cover with the lid, and let simmer for 45 minutes. Remove the pot from the heat and let sit for 30-45 minutes.

In a saucepan, heat balsamic vinegar to a boil and let simmer until the vinegar is reduced to half.

Cut off the octopus legs and set aside. Meanwhile, prepare your grill or heat a cast-iron skillet. Place the octopus legs directly on the skillet for about 4-5 minutes, just to give it a bit of char.

In a separate pan with a little olive oil, sauté the greens until just slightly wilted. You can also grill a wedge of lemon for serving.

Set the grilled octopus on a bed of sauteed greens then drizzle with olive oil dressing and balsamic reduction. Serve with a wedge of lemon.

Seasoned Italian Breadcrumbs

6 cups plain breadcrumbs
¾ cup grated parmesan cheese
¾ good olive oil
1 tbsp. finely chopped fresh garlic
½ cup chopped Italian parsley
Salt and pepper

Mix ingredients in a medium mixing bowl thoroughly so there are no clumps.

Keeps well in an airtight container in the refrigerator but best if used fresh.

Seasoned Cracker Meal

1 sleeve saltine crackers
Granulated garlic
Salt and pepper

Grind saltines in a food processor until fine. In a bowl, mix in the salt, pepper, and granulated garlic.

Crostini

Crusty Italian or French bread, a little less than ½ inch thick, cut at an angle
Olive oil, for drizzling

Preheat oven to 350° F.

Drizzle bread with olive oil, toast in prepared oven until crunchy.

Sauté 1 onion "Garlic" Chopped in olive oil with 2 carrots, 2 ribs celery, 1 potato, 1 zucchini all chopped; add 1 can Cannelini Beans drained, 1 can Garbanzo & 1 can Kidney Bean - 1 Lg. Can Tomato, 2 Beef Boulon Cubes & Water to Cover, Cook Gently 40 min - add Pasta & Pesto Cube - Cook 1' min more - Serve with Grated Cheese.

French Veg. Soup.

Chop 2 carrots, 2 potato, 2 ribs celery, 2 zucchini, 1 large onion put in large pot cover with water to cover add 1 chicken cube, salt, pepper, parsley. After 30 Min. - Mash with potato masher Continue cooking & Continue to mash while partially pureed, add ½ c. Butter & Serve.

Split Pea Soup

1 pk. split peas in large pot with 1 large onion chopped, chopped carrots 1, & 1 rib celery, chopped, cover with water, 1 chick

CHAPTER 2

Soups, Stews, & Salads

Mom's Minestrone Soup
Fresh Vegetable Soup
Split Pea Soup
Caesar Salad
No Mayo Cole Slaw
Cafe Fina Gazpacho Soup
Squid Salad
Lentil Soup
Beet Salad
David's Los Baños Lamb Stew

Mom's Minestrone Soup

Serves 4

Recipe by Josephine Mercurio.

About ten years ago, I called my mom and said, "Mom, can you give me a minestrone recipe?" It has been on the menu ever since. Customers love it.

2-3 tbsp. olive oil
2 stalks of celery, diced
1 carrot, peeled and diced
½ white onion, diced
1 clove of garlic, diced
28 oz. chicken broth
1 14.5 oz. can crushed tomatoes in juice
1 14 oz. can cannellini beans, strained
1 14 oz. can kidney beans, strained
¼ cup fresh chopped Italian parsley
¼ cup fresh chopped basil
Salt and pepper to taste
Pinch each of dried oregano and thyme
1 cup cooked elbow pasta
Optional, 1 tbsp. tomato paste
Optional, pesto for serving

Sauté celery, carrots, onions, and garlic in a soup pot with olive oil. When the vegetables are soft, add chicken broth, tomatoes, beans, parsley, basil, and thyme. Stir well and let simmer for about 30 minutes. Taste for salt and pepper. If you like a richer tomato flavor add a tablespoon of tomato paste and stir to incorporate. Add cooked pasta just before serving so the pasta doesn't overcook and become mushy.

Add a little pesto to each bowl as garnish before serving, if you like.

Fresh Vegetable Soup

Serves 4-6

Recipe by Josephine Mercurio.

2 carrots, peeled and diced
2 potatoes, peeled and diced, Russet works best but any will do
2 ribs celery, chopped
2 zucchini, chopped
½ large onion, finely chopped
1 chicken bouillon cube
Salt and pepper, to taste
Nice handful of freshly chopped Italian parsley
½ cup butter

Place the carrots, potatoes, celery, zucchini, and onion in a large pot. Add enough water to cover the vegetables. Bring to a boil.

Add bouillon cube, salt, pepper, and parsley. After 30 minutes mash with potato masher. Add the butter and let melt before serve.

Split Pea Soup

Serves 4-6

Recipe by Josephine Mercurio.

1 16 oz. package dried green split peas
1 cup salt pork, finely chopped
1 large onion, diced
2 carrots, peeled and diced
1 beef bouillon cube
Water
¾ cup cooked elbow pasta

In a large pot, place split peas, salt pork, onion, carrots, and the beef cube. Cover with water and cook for 40 minutes, then add pasta and continue cooking until pasta is done. Serve hot.

Caesar Salad

Serves 2-3

This is a shortcut version of the salad I used to make tableside, wearing a tuxedo, at Domenico's. It's a fading art.

Dressing:
3-4 salted anchovies
Salt
Fresh ground pepper
½ tsp. dried mustard
1 large clove of garlic
1 egg, coddled (or 1 tspb. mayonnaise)
½ cup extra virgin olive oil
¼ cup red wine vinegar
Juice of half a lemon
A couple dashes Worcestershire sauce

1 heart of baby Romaine lettuce, torn
¼ cup parmesan cheese
Croutons

In a wooden salad bowl, if possible (if not, a food processor will work), add anchovies, salt, pepper, mustard powder, and garlic. Mix until it turns into a paste.

Add the coddled egg (or mayonnaise) and mix thoroughly. If you're using the coddled egg, add extra virgin olive oil and continue mixing. Then add the red wine vinegar, lemon juice, Worcestershire sauce, and mix well. At this point the dressing should be thick.

Add the chopped hearts of baby romaine lettuce and toss. Add parmesan cheese and continue to toss; top with croutons to serve.

No Mayo Cole Slaw

Serves 6-8

This is a recipe that my Uncle John gave me when I was cooking a supper for Kenny Chesney at John Madden's recording studio. Chesney was doing a song called "The Boys of Fall" and had interviewed John Madden. This is something I wanted to do that was Southern cuisine.

½ head red cabbage, shredded
½ head green cabbage, shredded
½ cup horseradish
¼ cup sugar
½ cup extra virgin olive oil
¼ cup red wine vinegar
¼ cup apple cider vinegar
½ tsp. whole celery seed
1 can crushed pineapples, drained
3 cups shredded carrots

Mix all ingredients in a large mixing bowl. Let sit in the refrigerator for at least an hour. Mix well again and serve cold.

Cafe Fina Gazpacho Soup

Serves 4-6

This is a great hot weather soup, refreshing and light.

**3 cups peeled, diced cucumbers
1 yellow bell pepper, diced
1 green bell pepper, diced
2 stalks celery, diced
½ cup diced red onion
¼ cup chopped fresh Italian parsley
2 or 3 ripe tomatoes, diced
Pinch of ground cumin
Pinch of dried oregano
32 oz. tomato juice
3-4 oz. of your favorite Bloody Mary mix (Demitri's works best)
Salt and pepper to taste
Croutons, for serving**

Mix all ingredients in a bowl and let chill in the refrigerator until cold. Garnish with croutons and serve chilled.

Seasonal tomatoes from the Mercurio farm

Squid Salad

Serves 4-6

3-4 pounds squid, cleaned and cut into tubes and tentacles
Salt, for cooking
2 cloves garlic or more if you like, minced
2 ribs celery, diced
½ red onion, diced
A couple dashes lemon pepper
½ cup or so extra virgin olive oil
¼ cup red wine vinegar
½ cup fresh parsley, coarsely chopped

Put the chopped squid in a large pot and cover with salted water. Bring to a boil and boil for three minutes. Drain, and add garlic, celery, onion, lemon pepper, oil, vinegar, and parsley. Mix well.

Serve cold.

Photo from the Santa Rosalia festival in Monterey, circa late 1980s (left). Plaque on the statue of Santa Rosalia that overlooks the water and the Monterey Wharf (plaque, above; statue, opposite). Santa Rosalia is the patron saint of fishermen and of the city of Palermo, Sicily. My parents and family are big supporters of the festival.

Lentil Soup

Serves 6-8

Recipe by Josephine Mercurio.

½ lb. green or brown lentils
1 ½ quarts water
½ onion, minced
1 cup diced carrot
1 cup diced celery
1 beef bouillon cubes
1 15 oz. can tomato sauce
1 cup dry elbow macaroni
1-2 cups chopped Swiss chard
2 tbsp. pesto
Parmesan cheese, for serving

Rinse lentils and place in pot with the water, bring to a boil. Add the onion, carrots, celery, bouillon, and tomato sauce. Bring back to a boil. Reduce heat and let simmer for 40-50 minutes. Add pasta, Swiss chard, and pesto, and boil until pasta is cooked.

Serve hot with parmesan cheese.

Beet Salad

Serves 6-8

4 large beets
1 tbsp. dried thyme
¼ olive oil
½ cup of balsamic vinegar
½ head butter lettuce or 4 cups mixed greens
4 oz. goat cheese
Salt and pepper

To prepare the beets:

In a pot, cover beets with water an inch above the top of the beets. To the water, add thyme, salt and pepper, olive oil, and balsamic vinegar. Let boil until tender, 45 minutes to an hour. Add water if necessary to keep beets submerged in water. Remove from water and let cool until you can handle them. Peel the beets, cut into ¾ to 1-inch cubes, place in the refrigerator until chilled.

Serve beets over a bed of butter lettuce with goat cheese and either drizzle with balsamic vinaigrette or toss salad, which I prefer.

Season with salt and pepper to taste.

David's Los Baños Lamb Stew

Serves 6-8

For 19 consecutive years, we did annual BBQs for KCBS radio. This was one of the main attractions because my good friend David Sagousge, a tractor salesman in the central valley, would make this dish every year. He would cook it in a 30-gallon pot and it was one of his specialties.

3 pounds stewing lamb, cubed
1 cup water
3 large carrots, peeled and cut in 1-inch sections
1 yellow onion, diced
12 oz. tomato sauce
1 can beer, pick your favorite
1 cup white wine
2 garlic cloves, chopped
¼ cup freshly chopped Italian parsley
Italian seasoning to taste
Granulated garlic to taste
Season salt to taste
Pepper to taste
Crusty Italian bread, for serving

Place lamb in a large, covered pot (preferably a Dutch oven). Brown meat slightly to render fat. Add water. Bring to boil, skim fat, and stir. Keep heat high until meat is cooked.

Add remaining ingredients, except for Italian seasoning. Stir well.

Add seasonings in small amounts. Cover, bring to a boil. Stir. Simmer 15 more minutes.

Reduce heat to low, stir completely, and season to taste.

Simmer for one hour, stirring every 15 minutes. Check carrot tenderness. Add Italian seasoning to taste, be careful not to over season.

Stew is done when carrots are tender and lamb should begin to fall apart when poked with a fork. Remove from heat. Let stand 10 minutes. Serve hot with crusty Italian bread.

Boil 1 large Cauliflower chopped – Cook until tender, strain, saving water. In large frying pan in 3T olive oil add 4 cloves garlic chopped – brown lightly – add strained Caulflr, add salt, pepper, chopped parsley, & mash with fork – And cook gently 20 min – 2 Anchovies may be added with garlic.

Add pasta to Caulflower Water, when al dente, strain add 2T. butter & add to frying pan, & mix with grated Cheese. –

Pasta w/ Broccoli

Sauteed garlic in olive oil, add chopped Broccolli, ½ Can Tomato Sauce, add 4 Cups hot water, 1 Chicken Bouillon cube, Boil 20 min add 1 Cup. Salad macaroni, Serve w/ Cheese.

Fresh Tomato Sauce

Cut 4 Cups peeled chopped, peeled tomato in frying pan, add 4 chopped green onion 4 cloves garlic chopped, salt, pepper, ½ C Sugar Cook Slowly, add olive oil & 1 Cup chopped

CHAPTER 3

Sauces & Dressings

Marinara Sauce
Fresh Tomato Sauce
Fina's Finest BBQ Sauce
Mushroom Marsala Sauce
Caper Vinaigrette
Lemon Butter Caper Sauce
Mint Pesto
Tartar Sauce
Secret Sauce
Salmoriglio Sauce
Creole Mayonnaise
Louie Dressing
Seasoned Butter
Prosecco Mignonette Sauce
Creamy Italian Dressing
Balsamic Vinaigrette
Basil Cream Sauce

Marinara Sauce

Makes about two quarts

Recipe by Josephine Mercurio.

This is a basic marinara sauce. Marinara typically means no meat, just tomato and herb, which can be used in several of the recipes in this book. This is a typical recipe my mom used quite a bit, but she would change it from time to time depending on what she was using it for. Marinara is the base of many recipes—the key to good lasagna, for example, is starting with a good marinara sauce. It's important to note the difference between marinara and pizza sauce is that pizza sauce has more oregano, marinara has more basil.

Olive oil
1 white onion, diced
3 cloves garlic, chopped
2 28 oz. cans crushed pear tomatoes in juice
Pinch of dried oregano
1 tsp. dried basil
A pinch of dried thyme
¼ cup chopped fresh basil
1 tbsp. sugar
Salt and pepper to taste

Cover the bottom of the saucepan with olive oil, add diced onions and let soften over medium heat for 3-4 minutes. Then add chopped garlic, let cook for 7-8 more minutes stirring constantly. Add tomatoes and all herbs except salt and pepper. Let simmer over low heat for about an hour with the lid half on the pan. Then add salt and pepper to taste.

Fresh Tomato Sauce

Makes about a quart

Recipe by Josephine Mercurio.

**4 cups diced ripe Roma tomatoes
1 large yellow onion, diced
4 cloves garlic, chopped
Salt and pepper to taste
1 tsp. sugar
4 tbsp. olive oil
1 cup basil, chopped**

In a frying pan, add the tomatoes, onion, garlic, salt, pepper, and sugar. Cook gently, adding olive oil and 1 cup chopped basil after 15 minutes.

Serve with pasta and cheese; angel hair pasta is my favorite.

Midnight Roma and San Marzano tomatoes

Fina's Finest BBQ Sauce

Makes about a half gallon

When my dear friend John Madden asked me to help him test BBQ sauce recipes for his "Ultimate Tailgate Cookbook," we came up with this recipe. We had leftover pomegranate juice from the marinated lamb riblets from a previous dish we had tested. We tried a coffee-based BBQ sauce, but not everyone liked it. We tried a white BBQ sauce, which was good, but didn't knock your socks off and that's what we were going for. Out of all the sauces we experimented with in our "BBQ lab," as John called it, this is what we settled on.

2 cups chili sauce
2 cups ketchup
½ cup dark molasses
¾ tbsp. hot sauce
1 large onion, minced
½ cup lime juice
½ tsp. garlic powder
½ tsp. chopped fresh garlic
1 tbsp. dry mustard
½ cup apple cider vinegar
¾ cup light brown sugar
¼ cup Worcestershire sauce
1 cup dark beer, any will do
Fresh black pepper to taste
2 cups pomegranate juice
4 chipotle peppers

Mix all ingredients in a big stock pot, bring to boil and simmer for 20 minutes. Lasts a long time in the refrigerator.

Mushroom Marsala Sauce

Makes about 2 cups

½ stick butter, rolled in flour, divied
1 tbsp. sliced shallot
1 cup sliced mushrooms
⅓ cup dry marsala wine
1 cup heavy cream, optional
Salt and pepper
1 tbsp. finely chopped Italian parsley

Melt half the butter in a pan, add the shallots and mushrooms, cook until softened. Add the marsala and gradually stir in the cream, if using. Add the remaining butter, bring to a simmer, and cook for five minutes. Season with salt and pepper, to taste. After removing from heat and before serving, stir in the parsley.

Serve with stuffed veal rollatini or any white meat dish.

Caper Vinaigrette

Makes about 2 cups

½ cup ketchup
½ cup red wine vinegar
¾ cup olive oil
Salt and pepper to taste
¼ cup capers, drained
1 bay leaf
1 tsp. granulated garlic
1 ½ tsp. sugar
1 tbsp. fresh chopped parsley

Mix all ingredients well.

Great with whole artichokes, see page 6.

Lemon Butter Caper Sauce

Makes about half a cup

½ stick butter, divided
1 small clove garlic, minced
2 tsp. capers, drained
½ tsp. lemon zest
Juice of half a lemon
Flour to roll butter in
1 tbsp. cream
1 to 2 tsp. finely chopped parsley
Salt and pepper

Place half the butter in a pan over medium heat, once it is melted add the garlic, capers, lemon zest, and lemon juice. Cook until sauce slightly thickens then add the remaining butter, rolled in flour. Cook until the butter melts, stirring regularly. Add the cream and continue cooking until sauce thickens slightly. Turn off heat and stir in parsley and season with salt and pepper. Serve hot.

This sauce goes well with anything—veal, chicken, fish, etc.

Mint Pesto

Makes about 3 cups

1 tsp. minced garlic
1 cup freshly chopped parsley
1 cup freshly chopped mint
¾ cup good quality extra virgin olive oil
¼ cup white wine vinegar
Salt and pepper to taste

Mix all ingredients in a food processor until it is slightly thinner than traditional pesto.

Goes great with lamb.

Tartar Sauce

Makes about 3 cups

2 cups mayonnaise
Juice of half a lemon
1 tbsp. white wine vinegar
1 tsp. Worcestershire sauce
2 tsp. capers, drained
2 tsp. chopped Italian parsley
1 tbsp. diced yellow onion
½ tsp. granulated garlic
2 tbsp. sweet pickle relish
Salt and pepper to taste

Pulse all ingredients except salt and pepper in a food processor until everything is combined. Taste and add salt and pepper to liking as the Worcestershire sauce and capers add their own salt.

Enjoy with any squid dish; it also goes great with fish and chips.

Secret Sauce

Makes about 1 cup

Great on burgers.

½ cup ketchup
⅓ cup 1000 Island dressing
1 tsp. yellow mustard
Pinch of cayenne pepper
Pinch of onion powder
1 tsp. dried sweet Italian pepper powder (may be hard to find) or paprika

Mix all ingredients and let chill.

Salmoriglio Sauce

Makes about 1 ½ cups

1 cup crushed, canned pear tomatoes, or very ripe fresh tomatoes
2 tbsp. red wine vinegar
2 cloves garlic, minced
Good pinch of dried oregano
Juice of half a lemon
¼ cup olive oil
1 tbsp. freshly chopped Italian parsley
Salt and pepper to taste

Whisk all the ingredients together in a mixing bowl. Let sit at room temperature for at least an hour before serving.

This is the best with sardines.

Creole Mayonnaise

Makes about 1 ½ cups

1 cup mayonnaise
¼ cup finely chopped Italian parsley
1 tsp. finely chopped shallots
1 small clove garlic, minced
Juice of half a lemon
A couple dashes of tabasco sauce
1 tbsp. Dijon mustard
Couple shakes of Tony Chachere's Creole Seasoning
Freshly ground black pepper

Mix all ingredients well and let sit.

Great with Crabcakes, see page 14.

Louie Dressing

Makes about 3 cups

2 cups mayonnaise
1 tbsp. sweet pickle relish
¼ cup diced yellow onion
¼ cup freshly chopped Italian parsley
1 tbsp. red wine vinegar
Juice of half a lemon
¼ cup ketchup
Pinch of granulated garlic
½ tsp. sugar
Salt and pepper to taste

Mix all ingredients with a food processor or immersion blender.

Serve with any seafood salad.

Seasoned Butter

Makes about 2 ½ cups seasoning, enough to coat 2 sticks of butter

We serve seasoned butter balls at Cafe Fina and everyone loves them.

¼ cup garlic powder
¼ cup coarse salt
¼ cup black pepper
¼ cup oregano
¼ cup dry parsley
2 sticks butter, cut into half-inch cubes

Mix first five ingredients in a food processor for about 30 seconds. Roll cubed butter in dry herb mix and serve with fresh warm bread.

Prosecco Mignonette Sauce

Makes about 1 ½ cups

½ cup rice vinegar
½ cup white wine vinegar
1 tbsp. whole black pepper
1 tbsp. shallots, finely diced
½ cup dry prosecco

Mix all ingredients together well; let sit, preferably overnight.

Serve with fresh shucked oysters.

Creamy Italian Dressing

Makes about 3 cups

Works for any green salad.

2 eggs or 1 cup mayonnaise
1 cup extra virgin olive oil
1 cup canola oil
1 tbsp. garlic, minced
A couple dashes of white pepper
¾ cup red wine vinegar, adjust to taste
Salt to taste
¼ cup freshly chopped Italian parsley
Pinch finely chopped fresh oregano, or ½ tsp. dried oregano
1 tsp. sugar
1 tsp. lemon juice
A couple dashes of garlic powder
1 tsp. Worcestershire sauce

Blend all ingredients in a food processor except oils. Then gradually mix in oil with the food processor on.

Balsamic Vinaigrette

Makes about 2 cups

1 cup extra virgin olive oil
¼ cup orange juice
1 clove of garlic, finely chopped
½ cup balsamic vinegar
¼ cup finely chopped fresh Italian parsley
Salt and pepper to taste

Mix all ingredients and let chill.

Basil Cream Sauce

Makes about 2 cups

Olive oil for cooking
½ cup red onion, diced
1 clove garlic, minced
2 tbsp. white wine
½ cup freshly chopped basil
1 cup heavy cream
½ stick butter, rolled in flour
Salt and pepper to taste

Coat the bottom of a small saucepan with olive oil. Sauté onion and garlic in the olive oil, let brown. Add wine, basil, cream, and butter, turn down heat and let simmer, stirring constantly. Let reduce until it coats the back of a spoon, about 20 minutes. Do not let it boil, otherwise it will break.

Turn off heat and let cool to lukewarm, blend in a food processor and strain to get the solids out.

Goes well with grilled salmon.

Place 1 large flank steak, spread olive oil, sprinkle bread crumbs, served sliced Salami, & Quartered hard boil eggs. Roll tightly and tie with white Cotton String. Prep — add to Marinara Sauce — Cook gently 30 Min. & serve with Pasta or Ravioli. —

Pasta w/ Eggplant or Zucchini

Fry eggplant or Zucchini in peanut oil, Season with Salt, Pepper, & Grated Cheese. After boiling & straining pasta add fried Eggplant or Zucchini, fresh Basil, and Grated of Cheese.

Tortellini Al Panna

In large frying pan add 2 T Butter. add 4 slices Chopped prosciutti, 3 green onion Chopped — ¾ Cup Green peas, add 1 pt. ½ Cream — Let Simmer 15 - Gently — add dash Nutmeg - & lemon pepper. Serve over Tortelli.

CHAPTER 4

Pasta

Pasta Fina
Classic Clams in Linguini
Fettuccini Alfredo
Pistachio Pesto with Prawns over Penne
Pasta Gianna
Sautéed Swordfish with Eggplant and Mint over Fettuccini
Pasta Bolognese
Pasta alla Vodka
Salmon Pasta
Pasta Puttanesca
Lasagna with Sausage and Peas
Pasta with Peas
Pasta with Cauliflower
Pasta with Broccoli
Pasta with Eggplant
Squid and Peas over Fussili
Baked Pasta with Ricotta

Pasta Fina

Serves 4

This dish was invented at Domenico's by a woman from Capri, Italy, who made me lunch one day. I told her I was hungry and I wanted something different. She whipped this up for me and it was one of the best pasta dishes I had ever had with a butter and clam sauce. At Domenico's we called it Pasta Capri, after her hometown. When I brought it to Cafe Fina, I named it after my mother.

1 lb. dried linguini
2 tbsp. olive oil
½ cup salted butter, cubed
2 cups clam juice
3 cups diced tomatoes
1 ½ cups diced green onions
4 cups of baby shrimp
¼ cup dry white wine
1 cup sliced black olives
2 tbsp. finely chopped shallots

Cook linguini al dente in salted water and set aside, reserving some pasta water.

Add olive oil to pan to prevent sticking and combine all ingredients (except pasta) to the pan. Place over high heat, stirring occasionally. When butter has melted, cook for 1-2 more minutes then add pasta with a little bit of pasta water. Toss for one more minute and serve hot.

Classic Clams in Linguini

Serves 4

1 lb. dried linguini
3 lbs. fresh live clams
3 cloves garlic, minced
¼ cup salted butter
¼ cup freshly chopped Italian parsley
½ cup dry white wine

Cook linguini al dente in salted water, drain and set aside. Save some of the pasta water.

Cover the bottom of a frying pan with olive oil and add the whole clams (make sure none of the clams are open), cook for about 3 minutes. They will begin to open. Add the garlic and stir. When garlic begins to brown, add all the ingredients except pasta. When all the clams are open, add the pasta and a little pasta water and cook for another one or two minutes. Discard any clams that have not opened.

Serve in a big bowl with fresh cracked pepper.

Roxanne and I off the coast of Montenegro.

Fettuccini Alfredo

Serves 2

2 cups heavy cream
¼ cup salted butter
Couple dashes ground nutmeg
½ pound fettuccini, cooked al dente
½ cup grated parmesan cheese

Add the first three ingredients into a saucepan and mix well. Bring to a simmer and reduce heat slightly. Add cooked fettuccini. Let pasta cook in the cream sauce for about 1-2, minutes then add grated parmesan cheese. Continue mixing until the cheese has melted; the sauce should look like melted vanilla ice cream. If the sauce becomes too thick, add a little bit of the pasta water.

Divide evenly onto two plates, top with fresh ground pepper. The pepper is a must in this dish, it ignites it.

Pistachio Pesto with Prawns over Penne

Serves 2-3

When Roxanne, my partner, and I went on a Mediterranean cruise in 2019, we started in France with the bouillabaisse, then went on to Greece for whole roasted fish in Santorini, then to Naples, and ended in Sicily. The Prawns over Penne with Pistachio Pesto was the best thing that I ate on the trip at my cousin's good friend's restaurant in Furci Siculo in Sicily.

For the pistachio pesto:
½ cup pistachio flour or finely ground pistachios
½ cup olive oil
1 tsp. finely chopped fresh garlic
1 tbsp. grated parmesan cheese
¼ cup chopped fresh basil
1 tbsp. pine nuts
Salt and pepper

10 jumbo prawns (U15s)
½ lb. penne pasta, cooked al dente, reserve some pasta water

First make the pistachio pesto:

Mix all ingredients in a food processor until pasty. You don't want it too thick, thin out with olive oil if necessary. Set aside.

In a frying pan lightly coated with olive oil, place the prawns over medium heat for 1-2 minutes then turn over. Add the pistachio pesto and mix thoroughly; the prawns will continue to cook. Add cooked al dente pasta and ¼ cup of the pasta water. Continue to cook until all of the water is absorbed, it will create its own sauce from the starch in the pasta water.

Pasta Gianna

Serves 4

This is a no-brainer named after my granddaughter, born in April 2021. It's all my favorite things in a pasta.

Olive oil for cooking
4 Mom's meatballs, see page 112, cooked and chopped. If you don't have time to make them you can use 10 oz. ground beef, cooked.
2 links of sweet Italian sausage
4 cups marinara sauce, see page 50
½ cup of canned or frozen peas
¾ cup sliced mushrooms, cooked or canned
1 lb. rigatoni, cooked al dente
1 cup shredded mozzarella cheese
8 slices provolone cheese, about 4 oz.
Grated parmesan cheese, for serving
Red pepper, optional, for serving

Preheat oven to 350°F.

In a saucepan, add enough olive oil to coat the bottom, add sausage, and if using ground beef, add the ground beef as well. Cook until both meats are browned. If using meatballs, you will add those later.

Add 3 cups of marinara sauce, mix ingredients, then add peas, mushrooms, and cooked meatballs, if not using ground beef. Let simmer on low for about 5 minutes, then add the cooked rigatoni.

Stir all ingredients well, put pasta into an oven-proof dish. Cover with the mozzarella and provolone and bake in prepared oven until cheeses have melted. Serve with grated parmesan cheese.

Sautéed Swordfish with Eggplant and Mint over Fettuccini

Serves 4-6

This is a classic Sicilian dish.

Olive oil for cooking
1 tbsp. fresh chopped garlic
¼ cup freshly chopped Italian parsley, reserving some for serving
2 cups cherry tomatoes, cut in half
½ cup marinara sauce, see page 50
2 lbs. diced swordfish
3 cups diced eggplant, sautéed
¾ lb. fettuccini, cooked al dente, reserve some pasta water
Salt and pepper, to taste
10-15 fresh mint leaves, each torn in four pieces

Sauté garlic and parsley in olive oil until brown. Wait one minute, then add cherry tomatoes and marinara sauce. Then add swordfish and eggplant. Cook until swordfish is done (about 2 minutes), add cooked pasta with a little pasta water. Stir in mint at the end.

Serve with parsley and mint as garnish.

Pasta Bolognese

Serves 4-6

Recipe by Josephine Mercurio.

1 lb. fusilli pasta, cooked al dente, reserve some pasta water
2 medium onions, diced
3 carrots, peeled and diced
6 white mushrooms, washed and sliced
1 lb. ground beef
1 lb. ground sausage
1 cup red wine
Pinch oregano
4 cups marinara sauce, see page 50
½ cup heavy cream, optional
Salt and pepper to taste
Parmesan cheese, for serving

In a saucepan, sauté vegetables, beef, and sausage until meat has browned. Add wine, oregano, marinara sauce, and cream, if using. Simmer over low heat for 30 minutes, stirring occasionally. Add salt and pepper to taste.

Toss with prepared pasta and serve hot with parmesan cheese.

Pasta alla Vodka

Serves 4-6

Recipe by Josephine Mercurio.

Olive oil for cooking
1 stick butter
½ onion, diced
1 cup canned tomato strips or canned crushed tomatoes
¼ cup diced prosciutto
½ cup vodka
1 cup heavy cream
1 lb. penne pasta, cooked al dente, reserve some pasta water
½ cup parmesan cheese, plus more for serving
Salt and pepper, to taste

Cover the bottom of a saucepan with olive oil, add butter and diced onion. Cook until onion is lightly browned. Then add tomato strips and prosciutto, let cook for 5-6 minutes. Add vodka and cream, mix well, and cook for a few minutes. Then add cooked penne pasta and a little pasta water, tomato mixture and add parmesan cheese, salt, and pepper to taste, and cook a little longer.

Serve hot with parmesan cheese.

Salmon Pasta

Serves 4-6

We used to make this on the boat, one of the most satisfying dishes when we were done fishing. We'd make a big pot, enough for 8-10 guys.

Olive oil for cooking
1 small onion, minced
1 clove garlic, minced
2 lbs. salmon filet, skin removed
1 6 oz. can tomato paste
4-5 cups of water
Salt and pepper to taste
½ tsp. sugar
1 lb. dry fusilli
Pinch of dried basil
Pinch of dried oregano

In a large pot, sauté the onions and garlic in olive oil until lightly brown. Meanwhile chop up the salmon into one-inch squares. When onions are brown, add the salmon and stir constantly. Add tomato paste, water, salt and pepper to taste, and sugar. Bring to a medium simmer and add uncooked pasta. Cook until pasta is al dente, about 9 minutes but check for doneness. You may need to add more water.

Sprinkle basil and oregano before serving.

Pasta Puttanesca

Serves 4-5

Olive oil for cooking
½ tsp. freshly chopped garlic
3 salted anchovy filets
¼ cup large green olives, pitted and coarsely chopped
¼ cup kalamata olives, pitted and coarsely chopped
Pinch crushed red chili flakes, your preference on spice level
3 cups marinara sauce, see page 50
1 tsp. capers, drained
½ cup chopped fresh tomatoes
1 lb. cooked fettuccini, cooked al dente, reserve some pasta water
Parmesan cheese, for serving

Cover bottom of a saucepan with olive oil. Brown garlic then add anchovies. Stir to melt anchovies into the garlic; once incorporated add the rest of the ingredients, except the pasta and parmesan cheese. Bring to a simmer and let cook for 5-6 minutes, stirring occasionally.

Add cooked fettuccini with a little bit of pasta water and let the water absorb. Serve hot with parmesan.

Lasagna with Sausage and Peas

Serves 8-10

Classic lasagna recipe. When we have it on the menu, it sells out immediately. We can barely keep up.

You will need a 9 x 12 x 3" pan

For the lasagna:
2 lbs. sweet Italian sausage, removed from casing
2 lbs. ricotta cheese, strained
2 eggs, beaten
Salt and pepper
¼ cup fresh chopped Italian parsley
1 cup parmesan cheese, divided in half
6 cups marinara sauce, see page 50
1 box Barilla oven-ready lasagna noodles
1 cup peas, canned or frozen
1 lb. shredded mozzarella cheese

For the bechamel sauce:
1 cup milk
2 cups heavy cream
1 cube chicken bouillon
1 bay leaf
1 clove
½ yellow onion, chopped finely
Pinch white pepper

For lasagna, cook sausage and set aside.

In a mixing bowl, add ricotta, eggs, parsley, salt and pepper, and half the parmesan cheese. Mix until thoroughly incorporated.

For the bechamel sauce, combine all the ingredients in a saucepan, bring to a boil. Let reduce until it coats the back of a spoon, but not thick like gravy. Strain through a sieve and set aside.

Spread half a cup of marinara evenly on the bottom of the baking pan. Lay pasta sheets on the bottom, slightly overlapping. Spread half the ricotta over pasta noodles then sprinkle half of the peas, half of the sausage, and half of the mozzarella. Add another half cup of marinara on that, a half cup bechamel, and another layer of pasta and repeat the above filling. Add a third layer of pasta and top with marinara, and mozzarella. Cover with aluminum foil.

Bake in oven at 350°F for one hour. Let cool before serving. Top with more bechamel sauce when serving.

Pasta with Peas

Serves 2-4

Recipe by Josephine Mercurio.

Olive oil for cooking
1 onion, minced
1 clove garlic, minced
1 small can tomato sauce, 8-10 oz.
1 can peas, drained
2 chicken bouillon cubes
3 quarts water
1 cup small macaroni
Grated cheese, for serving

Sauté the onion with the garlic in the olive oil. Add the tomato sauce, peas, chicken bouillon cubes, and water. Boil for 20 minutes, then add the pasta and cook until pasta is cooked through.

Serve with grated cheese.

Pasta with Cauliflower

Serves 4-6

Recipe by Josephine Mercurio.

1 large cauliflower, chopped into 1-inch cubes
4 garlic cloves, minced
Olive oil for cooking
2 or 3 anchovy filets
Salt and pepper, to taste
1 lb. dry rigatoni
2 tbsp. salted butter
¼ cup grated parmesan cheese
¼ cup chopped fresh Italian parsley

Boil the cauliflower in salted water until tender, strain—saving water—and set aside. In a large frying pan add olive oil to coat the bottom and lightly sauté garlic and anchovies until evenly incorporated. Add strained cauliflower, salt and pepper, and mash with fork.

Cook gently for 20 mins.

Bring the cauliflower water to a boil. Once boiled, add pasta and cook al dente. Strain, and add the butter. Add the pasta to the frying pan with cauliflower mixture and stir in grated parmesan cheese. Stir in parsley and serve hot.

Pasta with Broccoli

Serves 2-4

Recipe by Josephine Mercurio.

2 cloves garlic, finely chopped
Olive oil for cooking
1 head broccoli, cooked or blanched and finely chopped
½ can tomato sauce
4 cups hot water
1 chicken bouillon cube
2-3 cups macaroni
Parmesan cheese, for serving

Sauté the garlic in olive oil. Add chopped broccoli and tomato sauce, then add the water and the bouillon cube, boil for 20 minutes before adding the macaroni, continue to simmer until pasta is cooked. Serve hot with cheese.

Pasta with Eggplant

Serves 4-6

Recipe by Josephine Mercurio.

1 large eggplant, peeled and sliced thinly
Salt and pepper, for seasoning
Olive oil for cooking
Parmesan cheese
1 lb. bucatini pasta
3 cups marinara sauce, see page 50

Soak the eggplant in salt water for a couple hours to get the bitterness out. Rinse and pat dry thoroughly.

Fry eggplant in a skillet, take out and place on paper towels to drain. Season with salt, pepper and grated cheese.

Boil pasta, al dente, strain and set aside, reserving some pasta water.

In the same skillet you used to fry the eggplant, place marinara and bring to a boil.

Add al dente pasta to sauce with reserved pasta water, bring back to a simmer then add eggplant and toss. Serve with grated cheese.

Squid and Peas over Fusilli

Serves 4-6

Living by the Monterey Bay, calamari is a staple. Besides having your typical fried calamari or calamari salad, this makes a great pasta dish.

2 lbs. squid, cleaned, tubes and tentacles, if possible

For the marinade:
1 cup white wine
1 small shallot, diced
Salt
Freshly ground pepper

For the pasta:
Olive oil
1 tsp. freshly chopped garlic
3 cups marinara sauce, see page 50
8 oz. shelled peas, frozen or canned and drained
¼ cup freshly chopped Italian parsley
1 lb. fusilli pasta, cooked al dente, reserve some pasta water

Cut squid into 1-inch rings, make sure beak and ink sac are removed. Add squid tubes and tentacles to bowl. Mix the marinade ingredients in a large bowl, add rings of squid and leave to stand for at least four hours in the refrigerator. Drain the calamari before adding to marinara sauce.

Heat oil in a skillet, add garlic. When the garlic begins to brown, add marinara sauce and peas and mix well. When the marinara mixture starts to simmer, add the drained calamari. Let simmer for 4-5 minutes, test one piece of calamari to make sure it's cooked but be careful not to overcook. When cooked, add pasta with a little bit of pasta water and let it absorb. Stir in parsley and serve.

Baked Pasta with Ricotta

Serves 6-8

1 lb. ricotta cheese, strained
2 eggs, beaten
3 tbsp. parsley, finely chopped
½ cup pecorino cheese
Dash nutmeg
1 lb. rigatoni pasta, cooked
3 cups marinara sauce, divided, see page 50
2 cups shredded mozzarella

Heat oven to 350°F.

In a small mixing bowl mix the ricotta, eggs, parsley, pecorino cheese, and nutmeg until thoroughly combined; set aside.

In a separate medium mixing bowl, toss the pasta with one cup marinara sauce.

Add one cup marinara sauce to the bottom of a 13 x 9-inch baking dish and spread to cover the bottom. Spread half the cooked and coated pasta in the baking dish, then spoon in the ricotta mixture over the pasta and spread into an even layer with a spatula or wooden spoon. Spread the remaining pasta over the ricotta layer and top with the remaining marinara sauce, spreading it over the pasta evenly. Sprinkle the mozzarella cheese on top; cover with foil and bake for 30 minutes.

Serve hot.

Squid Cioppino

In large pot Sauteed 1 large Chopped onion, add 4 Quater potatoes, 3 cups Chopped Squid, 1 Can Tomato Sauce - 1 Fish bouille - 1 Can water - Boil gently 20 Min or Until tender. Salt & pepper + Crushed hot pepper if desired.

Squid Salad

Put 4 Cups Chopped Squid in pot. Cover with Salted water, let come to boil + boil 3 Min - drain - add 2 clov garlic, 2 ribs celery - ½ Red onion - lemon juice, oil, Vinegar - Parsley - ¼ C. Italian dressing.

Breaded Squid

Dip Squid fillet in oil, then in Seasoned Bread Crumbs, grease Cookie Sheet - Lay Squid add Bread Crumbs + 1 Stick butter on the Squid - Bake at 375 - 15 - Min -

CHAPTER 5

Seafood

Cioppino
Squid Cioppino
Stuffed Calamari
Grilled Petrale Sole
Almond Crusted Roasted Sea Bass
Shrimp Burger
Salmon Burger
Rock Cod
Sanddabs
Breaded Squid
Fried Squid Steaks
Squid Balls
Rice with Squid
Baccala Fritters

Cioppino

Serves 6-8

If you like seafood, you will love cioppino. This is one of those recipes that we have served for over 40 years. The classic Italian seafood dish.

Olive oil
½ large onion, chopped
5 garlic cloves, chopped
1 cup red wine
4 cups clam juice
7 cups marinara sauce, see page 50
¼ cup fresh parsley, chopped
1 pinch saffron
1 cup fresh basil leaves, minced
24 clams, cleaned
24 mussels, cleaned
4 cups water
3 lbs. of white fish (rockfish, halibut, seabass, striped bass, etc.) cut into 2-inch pieces
12 large shrimp, shelled and deveined
1 Dungeness crab, cooked, cleaned, and cracked but leave shells on
3 lbs. squid, cleaned and cut into rings
Pepper to taste
Salt, but careful, clams can be salty

Cover bottom of a large pot with olive oil and sauté onions until browned. Add garlic, stirring occasionally until slightly brown. Add wine, clam juice, marinara sauce, saffron, half the parsley, half the basil, the clams, mussels, and water; bring to a boil. Cook covered over medium heat for 5 minutes. In this order, add the fish, shrimp, crab, and squid. Simmer covered for 5-10 minutes, until the clams and mussels open. Discard any unopened shellfish.

Garnish with remaining basil and parsley. Serve in a large bowl with crusty bread.

Squid Cioppino

Serves 2-4

Recipe by Josephine Mercurio.

1 small onion, chopped
3 cloves garlic, finely chopped
4 potatoes, peeled and quartered
2 lbs. squid, cleaned and chopped
1 28 oz. can chopped tomatoes
8 oz. clam juice
Salt and pepper, to taste
Water, for cooking (fill up the tomato sauce can), maybe
¼ cup chopped parsley
Crushed hot pepper, optional

In a large pot, sauté onion in olive oil and add potatoes. Sauté until onions are brown, about 20 minutes.

Add the can of chopped tomatoes, along with clam juice and salt and pepper to taste. Add squid, cooking for 3-5 minutes and checking for doneness. It's easy to overcook the squid and you do not want to. You may not need the water. The squid releases a lot of water, but this will depend on the squid.

Serve with crushed hot pepper, if desired.

Stuffed Calamari

Serves 6-8

This is another one of my favorite dishes that is for special occasions.

5 lbs. frozen calamari, tubes and tentacles, cleaned
1 link Italian sausage, chopped finely
¼ onion, diced
¼ cup raisins
1 tbsp. pine nuts
Olive oil for cooking
1 egg
1 cup ricotta cheese, strained
1 cup breadcrumbs
Salt and pepper, to taste
¼ cup chopped Italian parsley
5 cups marinara, see page 50
Pasta of your choice, for serving

Defrost calamari. When thawed, separate tubes from tentacles. Finely chop the tentacles and set aside.

Sauté sausage, onion, raisins, pine nuts, and tentacle pieces in olive oil for about ten minutes. Set aside to cool.

In a medium mixing bowl, beat the egg into the ricotta cheese. Add the cooked ingredients and breadcrumbs to the ricotta. Add salt and pepper to taste. If too dry, add a little bit of water. It should be the texture of a meatloaf. If available, place in a pastry bag (or use a Ziploc bag and cut off the bottom corner). Fill the squid tubes with the filling and thread closed with a toothpick.

Cook in a pot of marinara sauce for about 10-15 minutes.

Serve with the pasta of your choice.

Grilled Petrale Sole

Serves 2

Living in Monterey, this is a treat that you don't get everywhere. Petrale sole was called the Cadillac of sole by one of the owners of Monterey Fish Co.

2 eggs, beaten
2 ounces heavy cream
1 tbsp. freshly chopped parsley
Olive oil for cooking
½ stick butter

For the seasoned flour:
1 cup all-purpose flour
1 pinch salt
1 pinch pepper
1 pinch granulated garlic

1 lb. petrale sole filets

In a shallow bowl or pie dish beat the eggs and cream with the parsley; set aside.

In a frying pan over medium heat, coat bottom of pan lightly with olive oil, add butter.

In a shallow bowl or pie dish, mix the flour, salt, pepper, and seasoned garlic together then coat each side of the filets in flour then the egg mixture.

When butter is melted and just starts to bubble, reduce heat to low and add the filets. Check the bottom of the sole, when it is golden brown, flip the filet over and cook for another couple minutes until the other side is golden brown. Remove from pan and place on a paper towel to drain excess grease.

Serve on a warm plate with fresh lemon and a side of your choosing. Braised red cabbage goes well with this dish, see page 13.

Almond Crusted Roasted Sea Bass

Serves 4

When the squid run in Monterey Bay, usually there are white sea bass chasing them around. And if you're lucky enough to get one, or a piece of one, this is the way to cook it. You can also use Chilean sea bass if you're not a good fisherman.

For the almond crust:
¼ cup sliced almonds, lightly toasted and rough chopped
½ cup extra virgin olive oil
1 tsp. chopped fresh garlic
1 tbsp. chopped fresh Italian parsley
Salt and pepper; the salt is very important in this

4 7-ounce filets of sea bass, white sea bass is best
Salt and pepper, for seasoning
Olive oil for cooking

Preheat oven to 350°F.

While oven is heating, mix all ingredients for the almond crust in a food processor or mortar and pestle well—but not too fine—and set aside.

Season filets with salt and pepper. Place the fish on a lightly oiled baking sheet. Bake in prepared oven for about five minutes. Remove from the oven, top with almond mix and finish in oven for about 5 minutes, depending on how thick your filets are.

Serve with orzo pasta (see page 20) or your favorite fresh seasonal vegetables.

Shrimp Burger

Makes 2 burgers

This is a great alternative if you're a non-beef lover and you want a burger.

½ cup whole baby shrimp
1 cup chopped baby shrimp
2 eggs, beaten
½ cup breadcrumbs
Olive oil for cooking
Salt and pepper, to taste
Secret sauce, see page 55

Mix all ingredients well. Mold into 4 patties and pan fry in oil.

Serve on a hamburger bun with lettuce, tomato, pickles, and secret sauce.

Salmon Burger

Makes 4 burgers

We made this particular recipe with sockeye salmon. From fishing in Alaska for 19 years and bringing home several types of fish, we experimented with several different recipes and these sold very well.

1 ½ lbs. cooked salmon, deboned
½ cup mayonnaise
¼ cup sweet pickle relish
1 tbsp. dill pickle relish
2 tbsps. minced red onion
½ cup breadcrumbs
A couple shakes of paprika
Salt and pepper to taste
Olive oil for cooking
Secret sauce, see page 55

Mix all ingredients well. Mold into four patties and pan fry in olive oil.

Serve on a hamburger bun with lettuce, tomato, and secret sauce.

Rock Cod

Serves 2

A local staple I have been eating all my life. It can be prepared fried, BBQ'd, in cioppino or baked.

Olive oil for cooking and coating fish
1 ½ lbs. local rock cod filets
Salt and pepper
Seasoned Italian Breadcrumbs, see page 29
Tartar sauce, for serving, see page 55
Lemon wedges, for serving

Heat oven to 375°F.

Place some olive oil in a bowl and dip the fish in the oil. Add salt and pepper to each filet. Coat the filets with the seasoned breadcrumbs, giving a little pat to make sure the breadcrumbs stick.

Lightly coat a baking sheet with olive oil, and place breaded filets on it. Bake in oven for about 15-20 minutes or until fish is golden brown. Check fish, make sure it is thoroughly cooked but do not overcook. The transparency in the center should be gone.

Serve with tartar sauce and lemon wedges.

Sanddabs

Serves 2

In 2002, Cafe Fina was featured on Rachel Ray's "$40 a Day" on Food Network. She came to the restaurant with her crew and we filmed us making this dish.

10 sanddab filets
1 ½ cups of Seasoned Cracker Meal, see page 29
Olive oil for cooking
Freshly chopped parsley for serving
Lemon wedges, for serving
Tartar sauce or lemon butter caper sauce, see page 55 and 54

Coat the sanddabs with cracker meal and set aside.

Heat a griddle to medium-high or place a cast iron skillet over medium-high heat, coat lightly with olive oil. Have a spatula ready because the fish cook quickly. Place the sanddabs on the griddle, add a couple dots of olive oil between the filets. When the sanddabs are golden brown, turn them over and add a couple more drops of oil in between the filets. Cook until golden brown on both sides. They cook very quickly.

Best when served right off the griddle. Top with fresh chopped parsley and serve with either fresh lemons, tartar sauce, or lemon butter caper sauce. Serve with a side of your choosing.

Reprinted from "Rachael Ray: Best Eats in Town on $40 a Day" by Rachael Ray, Lake Isle Press, 2004. Photos by Mark Daniels.

Breaded Squid

Serves 2-4

Recipe by Josephine Mercurio.

2 lbs. squid filets, cleaned and patted dry
Olive oil for seasoning
Seasoned Italian Breadcrumbs, see page 29
Butter
Lemon wedges, for serving
Tartar sauce, for serving, see page 55

Heat oven to 400°F.

Cut squid tubes open; pound well to tenderize it.

Dip squid in oil, then in breadcrumbs. Grease cookie sheet with butter. Lay breaded squid and one dab of butter on each piece of squid. Bake for about 10 minutes, but it goes quick so watch it.

Serve with lemon wedges and/or tartar sauce.

Fried Squid Steaks

Serves 2-4

Recipe by Josephine Mercurio.

2 lbs. squid, cleaned and patted dry

For the seasoned flour:
1 cup all-purpose flour
1 pinch salt
1 pinch pepper
1 pinch granulated garlic

3 eggs, beaten for dredging
Seasoned Italian Breadcrumbs, or Seasoned Cracker Meal, for dredging, see page 29
Oil, for frying
Tartar sauce, for serving, see page 55
Lemon wedges, for serving

Cut squid tubes open; pound well to tenderize it.

In a shallow bowl or pie dish, mix the flour, salt, pepper, and seasoned garlic together.

Dip squid first in flour, then in beaten egg wash, then in seasoned breadcrumbs. Fry quickly in oil, drain on paper towels.

Serve with lemon wedges and/or tartar sauce.

Squid Balls

Serves 2-4

Recipe by Josephine Mercurio.

2 lbs. squid, cleaned and patted dry
Salt and pepper, to taste
2 cloves garlic, minced
¼ cup finely chopped Italian parsley
2 eggs, beaten
¼ cup grated parmesan cheese
2 cups Seasoned Italian Breadcrumbs, see page 29
Olive oil, for frying
2-3 cups marinara sauce, see page 50
1 lb. bucatini, cooked al dente

Place squid in food processer and chop until fine; place in a mixing bowl. Add salt, pepper, garlic, parsley, eggs, cheese, and seasoned breadcrumbs. Mix by hand until blended. Make into 1 ½" balls, about the size of golf balls, and fry in olive oil.

Heat marinara sauce in a saucepan, add squid balls and serve over pasta.

Rice with Squid

Serves 2-4

Recipe by Josephine Mercurio.

1 cup white rice
Olive oil for cooking
1 onion, minced
3 cloves garlic, minced
2 lbs. squid, cleaned, patted dry, and chopped finely
2 cups marinara sauce, see page 50
1 pinch saffron
1 cup canned peas, drained
1 fish bouillon dissolved in ½ cup water or ½ cup clam broth
Fresh basil, finely chopped

Sauté rice in olive oil until nice and brown. Add onion, garlic, and squid, and stir. Add the marinara, saffron, peas, and bouillon or clam broth and continue to cook, covered 10-15 minutes, or until liquid is absorbed.

Stir in basil and serve hot.

Baccala Fritters

Serves 2-4

Recipe by Josephine Mercurio.

1 filet dried cod, soaked then drained (see below)
2 eggs
Dash lemon pepper
Dash garlic salt
1 tsp. baking powder
Juice of one lemon
1 bunch fresh parsley, finely chopped
2 cups flour, may need more
½ cup water, may need more
Vegetable oil, for frying
Lemon wedges, for serving

To prepare the cod, you have to soak it in fresh water in the fridge, changing the water twice a day for three days. Boil cod until it flakes, check for bones when breaking apart; discard bones.

In a medium mixing bowl, beat eggs with water. Add cod, lemon pepper, garlic salt, baking powder, lemon juice, and chopped parsley and mix well. Add flour in increments, checking for smooth consistency. You may need to add more water.

Scoop about ¼ cup batter and flatten to a patty; repeat with the remaining batter. Fry in hot oil and drain on paper towels.

Serve with fresh lemon.

Joe DiMaggio and me at Cafe Fina in 1997.

& flake, ck for bones.

Beat 2 eggs with ½ cup water add lemon pepper, 1 tsp baking powder chopped parsley add flour about 2 cups — Ck for right consisty — You may need more water or flour. Fry in hot oil & drain on paper towels.

Patty Shells "Veal" Val-Vert

Brown 2 lbs Veal cut in small pieces in olive oil, In skillet. Sausepan Saute 1 large onion chopped add 3-4 lbs. Chopped Mushrooms, brown, add meat 1 cup dry white wine, 1 can Chicken Broth add 1 cup green olives — add salt, pepper + lid Simmer 40 min or until tender add 1 cup water with 2 T flour mixed, cook 2 min longer — Serve in Patty Shells, Mashed Potato or white Rice.

CHAPTER 6

Other Good Stuff

Mom's Meatballs
Cafe Fina Meatloaf
Sicilian BBQ Chicken
Italian Sausage
Italian Sausage Sandwich
Roasted Chicken with Potatoes, Carrots, and Celery
Bracciolli (Stuffed Flank Steak)
Stuffed Veal Rollatini
Rack of Lamb Dijon
Pomegranate Marinated Lamb Chops
Roasted Wild Duck
Mom's Breaded Chicken
Spiedini alla Siciliana (Grilled Beef Rolls)
Pizza Mia
Puff pastry shells with Veal (Veal vol-au-vent)

Mom's Meatballs

Makes 9-12 three-ounce meatballs

This recipe speaks for itself. It has been handed down from my maternal grandmother. When Italians come into the restaurant, they look at me amazed and say these taste just like their grandmothers'.

2 eggs
2 lbs. ground beef
4 sweet Italian sausage links, removed from casings
1 small clove of finely chopped or grated garlic
¾ cup breadcrumbs
½ cup grated Romano cheese
½ cup grated parmesan cheese
½ cup chopped Italian flat leaf parsley
½ cup water
Salt and pepper to taste, be careful with the salt as the cheese is salty
Marinara sauce, for serving, optional, see page 50

In a medium-sized mixing bowl mix all the ingredients, except the marinara sauce, together with your hands until everything is evenly mixed.

At the restaurant we grab an egg-size amount—like my grandmother would do—flatten it out, make it like a patty, pan fry it in a little oil and taste it to make sure it's just right. Adjust the parsley, cheese, etc. as necessary. Garlic should not be the main flavor here. Once you have it where you like it, use an ice cream scooper to make 3-ounce balls.

There are two ways to cook these, the best way is to fry them in a pan with a lot of oil. You have to constantly watch them, turning them to get the middle cooked and then finish them in a marinara sauce.

Or, put them on a sheet pan and bake them in the over at 350°F for 8-10 minutes. Check the centers to make sure they are cooked. Then, either add them to a warmed marinara sauce, or eat them as is, sprinkled with a little parmesan cheese.

Cafe Fina Meatloaf

Makes one meatloaf

This recipe is a good wintertime comfort food. One of my favorites—I love meatloaf.

2 lbs. ground beef
½ white onion, finely diced
1 cup Seasoned Italian Breadcrumbs, see page 29
1 packet Lipton onion soup mix
2 eggs, beaten
1 tbsp. Worcestershire Sauce
¼ cup fresh-chopped Italian parsley
1 pinch granulated garlic
1 carrot, peeled and shredded
½ cup water
Salt and pepper to taste
2 tbsp. ketchup, for brushing the meatloaf

Heat oven to 350°F.

Mix all the ingredients except ketchup. Pack into a bread loaf pan and lightly brush the top with ketchup. Cover with aluminum foil and bake for 1 hour in a water bath.* Remove foil and continue cooking for about 30 minutes or when internal temperature reaches 160°F.

Let sit for a few minutes, remove from pan. Cut and serve while still warm.

Place the bread loaf pan in a roasting pan and add an inch or two of water.

Sicilian BBQ Chicken

Serves 4-6

Food for Italians is sacred. Gathering around the table is an important part of every day and isn't taken lightly. We don't eat one-course meals, and we show our love by feeding people. But it doesn't have to be complicated, use what you have and do it right. This recipe is my grandmother's, but my grandfather Santo was in charge of the BBQ.

For Nana's marinade:
¼ cup olive oil
2 tsp. dried oregano
3 cups white wine
8 large garlic cloves, sliced thinly
1 tbsp. soy sauce
2 tbsp. ketchup
Dash of lemon pepper
Freshly ground pepper, to taste
Salt, to taste

12 chicken leg quarters, keeping legs and thighs connected
Salt and pepper, for seasoning

In a large jar, mix the marinade ingredients, mix well and let stand at room temperature for one hour.

Make a very hot charcoal fire or preheat gas grill. Salt and pepper the chicken pieces. Place chicken on grill, skin-side up. When cooked halfway, turn over and cook the other side until it is just done, but not more than that.

Place the grilled chicken in a large roasting pan. Pour marinade over the chicken evenly. Cover the pan with foil and/or lid, sealing tight. Place pan on grill or in oven for 30 minutes at 350°F. Serve hot.

Italian Sausage

Makes 40-50 links

This recipe was given to me by a man we called Prosciutto Pete. His real name was Peter Radich, he was Croatian, and his son, Kevin the Rat, was a sports reporter on KCBS radio. Knowing I was Italian, and he being Croatian, he invited me and my dad to his house to learn to make sausage. We showed up at 7:00 in the morning and were immediately taken to the wine cellar and given shots of homemade brandy, along with homemade prosciutto, some of the best I've ever had. We spent the morning making the sausage. When we were all done, about a dozen guys, including John Madden, had a feast of pasta, sausage, and homemade wine.

10 lbs. coarse ground pork, a ⅜ chili grind works great
3 tbsp. salt
1 ½ tbsp. whole fennel seed
1 ½ tbsp. whole anise seed
1 tbsp. granulated garlic
1 tbsp. black pepper
1 tbsp. dried sweet Italian pepper, or paprika if you can't find it
1 cup zinfandel
Sausage casings
*optional, for hot sausage add 1 tsp. crushed red chili peppers, or more depending on your preference

Mix ingredients well. Stuff into casings or can be made into patties for frying or barbecuing. Sausages freeze well.

It's best if you refrigerate the sausage for at least 48 hours before freezing or cooking.

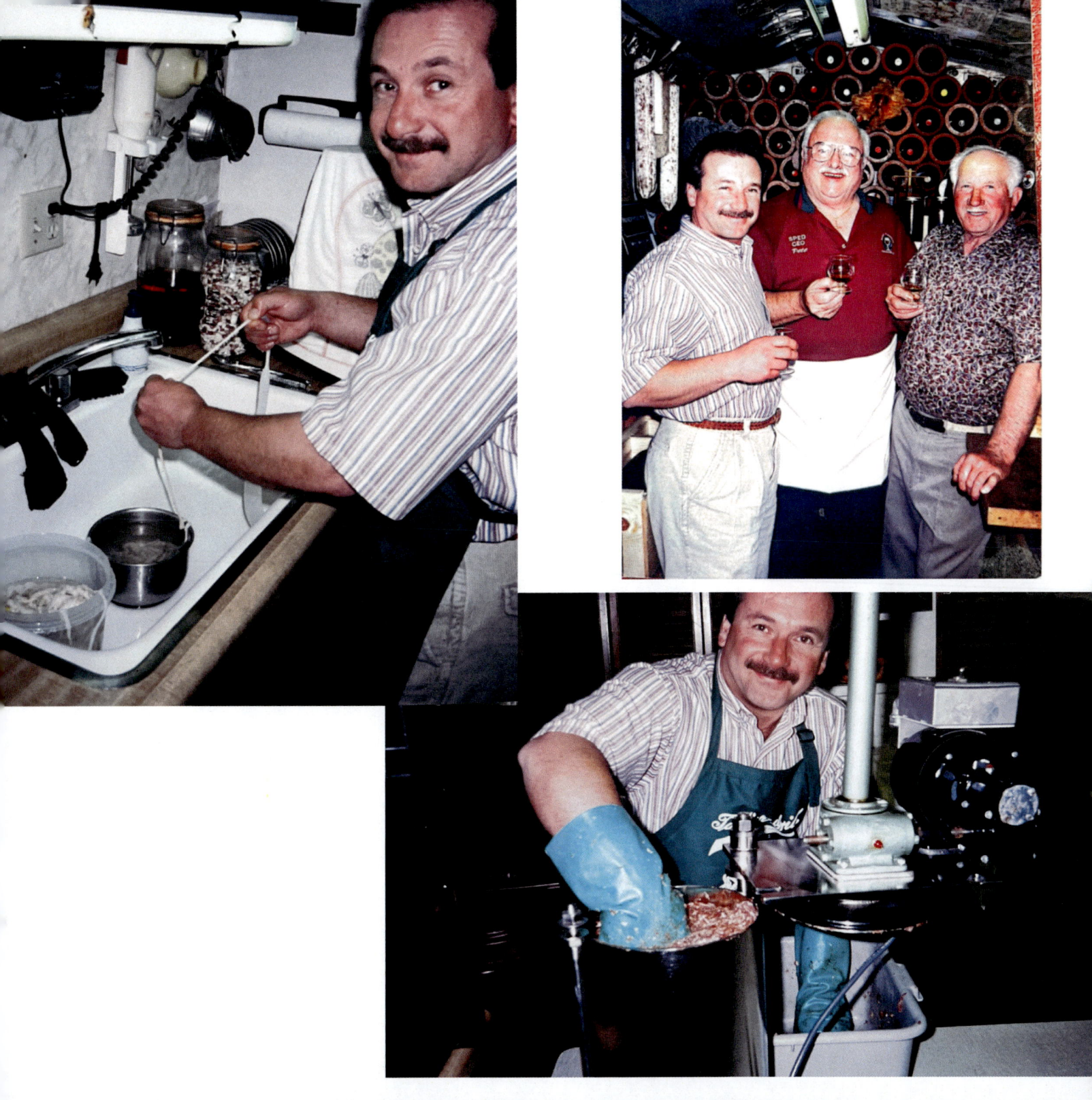

Italian Sausage Sandwich

Serves 8-12

4 large onions, julienned
3 red bell peppers, julienned
½ tsp. granulated garlic
Olive oil
Salt and pepper, to taste
½ cup white wine
8-12 Italian sausage links, mild or hot
6-8 French rolls
Red wine vinegar, for brushing the sausages

In a large frying pan sauté the onions, bell peppers, and garlic in olive oil with the salt and pepper. Toss them occasionally until soft, I like them a bit charred. After 5 minutes add wine and let simmer for 5-10 minutes. Set aside.

Prepare a charcoal fire or preheat grill. Place sausages on grill at medium heat, cooking both sides completely. When the sausages are cooked through, about 10 minutes, put French rolls on the grill for 1 minute. Put one or two sausages per roll, add onions and peppers. Brush the sausages with a little vinegar and serve.

Roasted Chicken with Potatoes, Carrots, and Celery

Serves 4-6

1 whole large chicken, 3-4 lbs., giblets removed
1 onion, sliced
4 stalks of celery, diced
2 large carrots, peeled and coin-cut
2 potatoes, washed, skin on, and quartered
1 cup white wine
2 cups water
1 tsp. dried oregano
1 tsp. chopped garlic
Salt and pepper to taste
1 cup marinara sauce, see page 50

Heat oven to 375°F.

In a large roasting pan, place the chicken, breast side up, and all the ingredients except marinara around it. Pour the marinara sauce over the chicken. Let bake until the top browns. Reduce temperature to 350°F, cover with foil and continue baking until internal temperature is 165°F, about 45 minutes to an hour.

Baste with drippings before serving.

Braccioli (Stuffed Flank Steak)

Serves 8

This is a classic Southern Italian dish that is served for special occasions. It is slowly cooked in marinara sauce, homemade is the best, and served over pasta. It is the ultimate Italian family meal.

2 lbs. flank steak
Salt and pepper
Garlic powder
Olive oil, for drizzling
¼ lb. salami, sliced
¼ lb. pepperoni, sliced
½ cup parmesan cheese
½ cup mozzarella cheese, shredded
½ cup breadcrumbs
4-5 hard boiled eggs, peeled and whole
Butcher's string
¼ cup red wine
Marinara sauce, see page 50
Penne or rigatoni pasta, cooked al dente

Pound the flank steak so that it's thin (about ¼-½ inch thick). Season with the salt, pepper, and garlic powder, drizzle with a little olive oil. Lay pounded flank steak on a large flat surface or sheet pan; add salami, pepperoni, parmesan cheese, mozzarella, and breadcrumbs. Make sure everything is flat and uniformly distributed from edge to edge. Line the hardboiled eggs, end to end, about a third of the way down and carefully roll the flank steak, with all the seasonings, around the eggs. With butcher's string, carefully tie the middle first, then the ends tightly so the cheese doesn't melt out, and a few tied in between. In a large saucepan, cover the bottom with olive oil, brown the meat on each side. Remove from heat and set aside.

Turn the heat up and deglaze the pan with red wine. Add *braccioli* back to the saucepan and add enough marinara sauce to cover most it. Simmer slowly for 2-3 hours, covered, checking frequently to not burn the meat on the bottom of the pan.

When it's done, slice it like you would a loaf of bread, about ¾ of an inch thick, and serve over pasta.

Stuffed Veal Rollatini

Serves 4

Recipe by Josephine Mercurio.

My mom used to only make this a couple times a year. It takes time, but it's well worth it.

8 veal cutlets, pounded (each one should be about 3-4 oz)
Olive oil for cooking
Salt and pepper to taste
8 slices prosciutto
1 cup diced provolone
½ cup chopped Italian parsley
¼ cup lightly roasted pine nuts
8 basil leaves, sliced thinly
Flour for dredging
3 eggs, beaten
Mushroom marsala sauce, see page 53

Heat oven to 350°F.

Lay the veal cutlets on a sheet pan. Drizzle each cutlet with a little olive oil, add salt and pepper to each.

Divide the prosciutto, provolone, parsley, pine nuts, and basil evenly on the eight cutlets. Roll and thread closed with toothpicks or skewers as tight as possible so the filling doesn't come out when cooking.

Roll each rollatini in flour and then egg. Pan fry in olive oil until browned on all sides. Finish in oven at 350°F, check with a meat thermometer until center is at 150°F.

Plate and serve immediately with mushroom marsala sauce.

Rack of Lamb Dijon

Serves 2-4

2 racks of lamb, about 6 bones each, flap on (the layer of fat that normally covers the rack)
1 cup breadcrumbs
Salt, pepper, and granulated garlic to taste
½ cup Dijon mustard, or enough to cover rack

Heat oven to 350°F.

Peel flap back on racks of lamb but do not cut off. Season racks with salt, pepper, and granulated garlic. Place on hot BBQ until evenly seared but not cooked. This gives it a nice smoked flavor.

Remove from fire, peel flaps back and coat with Dijon mustard, sprinkle evenly with breadcrumbs then replace flap. Finish in oven at until internal temperature reaches 135-140°F. Remove and discard flap.

Slice at the bone and serve with mint pesto (see page 54) and sides of your choice; roasted potatoes work well with this dish.

Pomegranate Marinated Lamb Chops

Serves 4-6

This is another recipe from John Madden's tailgate cookbook that was a home run and I still love making to this day.

4 lamb chops

For marinade:
2 cups pomegranate juice
2 tbsp. chopped fresh garlic
Salt and pepper to taste
½ cup fresh chopped mint

Mint pesto for serving, see page 54

Stir all ingredients together and set aside.

Place lamb chops in marinade, cover, and refrigerate for at least 8 hours.

Cook on a grill until internal temperate is 135-140°F.

Serve with mint pesto.

Roasted Wild Duck

Serves 8-12

This is a recipe I got 40 years ago from a good friend of mine Anthony "Red" Gangi. He was one of the co-owners of Gangi Brothers tomato processing in downtown San Jose, which eventually moved to Riverbank in the Central Valley. Knowing I was an avid duck hunter like him, he shared this recipe with me, which turned out to be one of the best recipes that I have for wild duck.

Marinade:
4 cups soy sauce
½ cup brown sugar
1 tbsp. chopped garlic
1 bay leaf
1 tsp. coarse black pepper
1 12 oz. can frozen orange concentrate, thawed
¼ cup thinly sliced ginger root

4 big ducks or 8 small ducks (teal), cleaned

Heat oven to 500°F.

Mix all ingredients except ducks together, making sure brown sugar and orange juice are completely dissolved.

Place ducks, breast side down in marinade and refrigerate for at least 8 hours, but 24 is better, turning every 4 hours.

Roast ducks in deep roasting pan because ducks have a lot of fat. Cook in prepared oven for 20 minutes for small ducks and 30 minutes for big ducks. Do not overcook, must be medium rare.

Mom's Breaded Chicken

Serves 4-5

Recipe by Josephine Mercurio.

This is another dish that my mom made that is a great go-to warm or cold. My mom always made a big dish of this for us when we were going duck hunting for the week and my friends from Ohio were here. This is always something you could grab at any time of the day and it is delicious.

4 cups Seasoned Italian Breadcrumbs, see page 29
1 cup parmesan cheese
2 tbsp. olive oil
2 cups flour
Salt and pepper
8-10 pieces chicken, legs and thighs, skin on is better
6 eggs, beaten in a shallow dish
Butter for topping

Heat oven to 375°F.

In a medium sized mixing bowl, place the breadcrumbs with the parmesan cheese and olive oil; mix thoroughly until there are no clumps.

In a separate bowl, mix flour with salt and pepper. Set aside.

Pat chicken pieces dry.

Dip the chicken pieces in flour, then eggs, then breadcrumb mix, in that order. Tap excess off and place on a baking sheet, topping each piece with a pea-size piece of butter, or more if you like. Cook in oven at 375°F for 40-50 minutes, turning over once halfway through until light brown and edges are crispy.

Puff pastry shells with Veal (Veal *vol-au-vent*)

Serves 6

Recipe by Josephine Mercurio.

2 lbs. veal, cut in small cubes
Butter, for cooking
1 large onion, chopped finely
¾ lb. mushrooms, sliced
1 cup small green olives, pitted
½ cup dry white wine
1 cup chicken broth
½ cube butter, rolled in all-purpose flour
Salt and pepper to taste
6 puff pastry shells, prepared per instructions on the package

Brown veal pieces in butter. In separate saucepan, sauté the onion until nice and brown. Add the mushrooms, olives, veal, white wine, and chicken broth.

Let simmer until tender, 30-40 minutes. About 25 minutes into simmering, add the butter that's rolled in flour and stir constantly until melted to thicken the sauce.

Serve in puff pastry shells, with mashed potatoes or white rice.

Spiedini alla Siciliana (Grilled Beef Rolls)

Serves 6-8

Recipe by Josephine Mercurio.

Another one of my mom's great recipes. I loved this when she made it.

For the spiedini:
- 16 raw beef slices, cut from the top round or flank, 4-6 inches, 1/8-1/4 inch thick for each slice, about 2 ½ lbs.
- 16 large bay leaves
- 3 cups shredded mozzarella
- 2 tbsp. pine nuts
- 8 slices prosciutto, 1/16 inch thick, finely chopped
- Salt and pepper
- 2 ½ cups Seasoned Italian Breadcrumbs, see page 29
- ¼ cup green onion, thinly sliced, both white and green parts
- Olive oil
- 6-8 wood or metal skewers. If using wood, soak in water to prevent ends from burning

For the basting sauce:
- 5 large cloves garlic, chopped
- 1 cup water
- ¼ cup olive oil
- 1 tsp. oregano
- Salt and pepper

First make sauce. Over medium heat in a small saucepan, add garlic, water, olive oil, oregano, salt and pepper to taste. Bring to a boil and remove from heat. Set aside.

Next, prepare a charcoal fire or preheat a gas grill.

Place the beef slices between two pieces of wax paper and flatten with a mallet or the side of a cleaver until they are about 1/16 inch thick. If using dry bay leaves, soak them in water.

Mix together green onions, breadcrumbs, mozzarella, pine nuts, prosciutto, and salt and pepper. Place a tablespoon or so of mix on each beef slice. Carefully roll up the slices and secure with two skewers, about 2 inches apart, skewering a bay leaf through to separate the rolls. Eight rolls should fit on a 14" skewer. Alternate roll, bay leaf, roll, bay leaf, etc.

Cook on the prepared grill for 2-4 minutes on each side, until the meat is cooked through.

Brush or spoon sauce over beef rolls and serve hot.

Pizza Mia

Makes one 8-9" pizza

This was one of my favorite pizzas that I had when I was in Sicily. I just had to name if after my second granddaughter when she was born in May 2023.

1 eight-ounce ball of pizza dough, store-bought is fine
Olive oil, for drizzling
Garlic salt
2 ounces shredded mozzarella cheese
2 ounces provolone cheese
4-6 slices of prosciutto
6-8 sundried tomatoes, best if you use sundried tomatoes soaked in oil, lightly taping off excess oil before adding to pizza but do not pat dry
2 tbsp. coarsely chopped pistachios
Fresh basil

Heat oven to 450-500°F or prepare pizza oven.

Roll out the pizza dough to 8 or 9 inches. Drizzle with olive oil and sprinkle with garlic salt. Cover with the mozzarella and provolone. Lay out the prosciutto over the cheese to cover the entire pizza.

Bake in a pizza oven or very hot oven until pizza is 95% cooked.

Remove from oven and add sundried tomatoes. Return the pizza to the oven and bake for 1 minute. Be sure to not burn the sundried tomatoes.

Remove from oven and cut into 6 or 8 slices. Add the pistachios, then fresh basil on top and serve hot.

Lentil Soup

Rinse 1 lb lentils and put in
pot with 5 qts water, add 1 cup each
of onion, Carrots, Celery, 2 beef Bouillon Cubes,
1 small Can Tomato Sauce, let simmer about
50 min – add pasta – 2 cup chopped Swiss chard,
(1 Pesto Cube) – boil another 10 min – Serve
with Italian cheese.

Tortellini Soup

Boil 1 pt Tortellini until tender,
Drain and add to 1 large Can Swanson
Chicken Broth, add 1 cup green peas –
1 C. green Onion, add 2 cups chopped
½ Escarole – add 2 beaten eggs with
½ C. grated cheese – Remove
from Heat.

Pasta w/ Peas

Saute 1 onion w/ 1 clove garlic in
2 T. olive oil, add 1 Small Can tomato
Sauce + 1 Can peas, drained, 2 chicken
Bouillon Cubes, add 3 qt. water, boil until

CHAPTER 7

Dessert & Drinks

Italian Ricotta Cookies
Dipping Sauce for Strawberries
Italian Ricotta Cheesecake
Cannoli
Ultimate Chocolate Cake
Sesame Cookies or Queen's Biscuits (*Biscotti di Regina*)
Biscotti
Bread Pudding
Lemon Cheesecake Bars
Homemade Limoncello

Italian Ricotta Cookies

Makes 30 cookies

Recipe and photo by Kathryn Donangelo.

For the cookies:
½ cup unsalted butter, softened
1 cup granulated sugar
1 large whole egg
7.5 oz. whole or part skim ricotta, strained
2 tbsp. lemon juice
2 tsp. lemon zest (zest from one whole lemon)
¾ tsp. almond extract
1 tsp. vanilla extract
2 ½ cups all-purpose flour
1 ½ tsp. baking powder
¼ tsp. salt
Sprinkles, optional

For the glaze:
2 cups powdered sugar
3-4 tbsp. milk
¼ tsp. vanilla extract
¼ tsp. almond extract

In a large bowl with an electric or a stand mixer, cream together the softened butter and sugar until smooth.

Add the egg, ricotta cheese, lemon juice, lemon zest, and vanilla and almond extracts. Mix until all of the ingredients are combined and smooth. Be sure to scrape down the sides of the bowl periodically.

continued on next page

In a medium bowl, whisk together the flour, baking powder, and salt. Add the flour to the wet ingredients in three increments. Be sure to mix together in between each addition. Mix until just combined, do not overmix. Cover the mixing bowl with plastic wrap and refrigerate for at least an hour, or overnight.

When ready to bake, preheat oven to 350° F. Line two baking sheets with parchment paper or silpat mats. Using a mini ice cream scoop, scoop the cookie dough balls or measure out two tablespoons of dough. Place cookies on the baking sheet 1 ½ inches apart. Bake for 11-12 minutes. The cookies will not turn golden brown, but the bottoms will.

Let the cookies cool on the baking sheet for a few minutes before transferring to a cooling rack to cool completely.

When the cookies are completely cooled, whisk together the powdered sugar, milk, and extracts until smooth. Spoon the glaze on top of each cookie and top with sprinkles if you're using. Let cookies set for a few minutes and enjoy!

Dipping Sauce for Strawberries

Makes about a cup and a half of dipping sauce

This was given to me by my good friend, Jerry Avachian, who passed away from cancer. This is a super simple recipe that goes so well with strawberries. Jerry was my duck-hunting partner and great friend; he was always there for me.

1 cup sour cream
¼ cup honey, (sage honey if available)
2 oz. amaretto

Mix all ingredients well. Serve with fresh strawberries.

Italian Ricotta Cheesecake

Makes one 9" cheesecake

3 lbs. ricotta cheese, strained
Zest of one orange
1 tbsp. flour
1 cup sugar
¼ cup sour cream
1 tbsp. vanilla extract
¼ cup whipping cream
8 eggs

Graham cracker crust:
9 whole graham crackers, 1 sleeve, crushed or pulverized
⅛ cup sugar
¾ stick butter, melted

Hot water, for baking in a *bain marie* (water bath)

Glaze:
1 egg white
1 oz. amaretto

Heat oven to 425°F.

Bring about a gallon of water to boil.

While the water heats, in the bowl of a standup mixer, place the ricotta, orange zest, flour, sugar, vanilla, and whipping cream. Beat on medium-low for 10 minutes, adding the eggs, one at a time. If you are using a mixing bowl and hand mixer, keep the speed low but beat until your mixture is light and fluffy.

Coat the edges of a 9" springform pan with olive oil.

In a medium mixing bowl, mix the graham crackers, sugar, and melted butter until it's all incorporated. Press the graham cracker mixture into the base of the prepared springform pan.

Pour the batter into the springform pan and tap it on the counter to release any air bubbles. Place the pan inside a roasting pan and carefully pour hot water into the roasting pan. Be sure not to splash any hot water into the cheesecake.

Bake in the hot oven for 15 minutes, then reduce heat to 275°F and continue to bake for one hour.

While the cheesecake bakes prepare the glaze by beating an egg white into 2 oz. of amaretto.

When the cake is done, remove from oven and water bath. Let cool completely before covering with plastic wrap and placing in the refrigerator to cool at least six hours, if not overnight.

When the cake is fully chilled, remove from the springform pan, top with glaze and serve.

Cannoli

Makes about two dozen cannoli

For as many Italian cooks there are in the world, there are that many cannoli recipes. Cannoli is a traditional Sicilian dessert that is found in most restaurants and all Italian pastry shops.

For the shells:
4 cups all-purpose flour
4 tbsp. sugar
Zest of 1 lemon
4 tbsp. cold butter
2 whole eggs
¼ cup marsala wine
Cannoli forms
Oil for frying

For the filling:
3 lbs. ricotta cheese, strained
2 cups powdered sugar
¼ cup mini chocolate chips
½ cup candied citrus, chopped finely
1 oz. Galliano
2 tsp. vanilla extract
Powdered sugar for serving

Maraschino cherries for garnish

Line platters with paper towels, set aside.

For the shells: Mix eggs and wine together, set aside. In a large bowl mix the flour, sugar, and lemon zest and then cut in the butter. Make a crater in the flour mix and add the egg and marsala mixture. Mix well until the dough is soft and smooth, cover and let rest in the refrigerator for an hour.

Begin to heat your frying oil.

As oil heats, you the dough for frying. On a floured surface, roll out some of the dough with a rolling pin very thin. Using a small coffee can, squeezed to the form of an oval, about 3 x 4 inches, cut out ovals of dough.

Wrap around the cannoli forms and using a touch of water, press the edges to seal the cannoli around the form. Once oil gets to 350°F, it's ready, fry until golden but not burned. Remove from hot oil with tongs; grab form with pliers and wrap towel around the cannoli, slide off onto prepared platters to drain.

For the filling, in a large bowl, mix all the ingredients together.

When the shells are cooled, stuff with the ricotta filling, dust with powdered sugar and serve.

Only stuff the shells you will be eating so they stay crisp. They keep well in an airtight container for up to a few weeks. The ricotta filling will last about 3 days in the refrigerator.

Ultimate Chocolate Cake

Makes 2 cakes

Recipe by Virginia Madden.

Every year that we did the KCBS radio BBQ at John's sound stage, we were in charge of all the main and side dishes while Virginia was responsible for the desserts. She makes the best chocolate cake I've ever had.

For the cake:
2 cups chocolate chips
¼ lb. butter
½ cup water
4 eggs, separated
2 cups cake flour, sifted
1 ½ cups sugar
1 tsp. baking soda
1 tsp. baking powder
1-2 tsp. vanilla
16 oz. sour cream

For the frosting:
1 stick butter
2 cups chocolate chips
½ pint whipping cream
1 ½ cups powdered sugar
1 tsp. vanilla

For the cake:

Preheat oven to 350°F.

Spray two Bundt pans with cooking or vegetable oil, then flour both pans.

Place chocolate chips, butter, and water in a microwave safe bowl and microwave for two-three minutes, until chips and butter melt. Mix until well incorporated.

Separate eggs, placing yolks in small bowl and whites in mixing bowl. Beat whites until stiff peaks form.

In a mixing bowl, combine flour, sugar, baking soda, and baking powder. Add yolks, one at a time to the chocolate mixture and mix until smooth. Add sour cream and vanilla, mix well.

To the chocolate mix, add about a third of the egg whites, folding in gently. Fold in a third of the flour mixture. Repeat this in two more additions of flour mixture, and egg whites. Do not overmix.

Divide mixture evenly into the two Bundt pans. Bake for 50-55 minutes or until toothpick inserted in center comes out clean. You do not want this cake to be dry.

For frosting:

Mix butter, chocolate chips, whipping cream, and powdered sugar in double boiler on low heat. Stir until all is melted and smooth. Add vanilla. Stir and keep warm.

Assembling the cake:

Remove cake from oven and let cool 5 minutes in the pan. Turn upside down, remove pans. While cake is still warm, pour frosting over cakes and fill centers with frosting.

Sesame Cookies or Queen's Biscuits (*Biscotti di Regina*)

Makes about 6 dozen

This is my Aunt Betty's recipe. They are the best.

4 cups all-purpose flour
1 cup sugar
1 tablespoon baking powder
¼ tsp. salt
1 cup shortening
2 eggs, slightly beaten
½ cup milk
¼ lb. sesame seeds

Heat oven to 375°F.

Lightly grease two cookie sheets and set aside.

Into a medium bowl, sift together the flour, sugar, baking powder, and baking soda.

Cut the shortening in with a pastry blender.

Stir in the eggs and milk to make a soft dough; be sure to mix thoroughly.

Break dough into small pieces and roll each piece between palms of hand to form rolls about 1 ½ inches long. Flatten rolls slightly and roll in sesame seeds.

Place on cookie sheet and bake 12-15 minutes or until cookies are slightly brown on top.

Biscotti

Serves 4-6

Kathy and Rocco DiMaggio have been my lifelong friends. This is Kathy's classic biscotti recipe. She made these for my daughter's wedding.

⅓ cup brandy
1 ½ tsp. anise extract
1 tsp vanilla
3 tbsp. anise seed
2 cups sugar
2 sticks butter, at room temperature
4 eggs
4 ½ cups flour
4 teaspoons baking powder
1 cup whole toasted almonds

Preheat oven 350°F.

Place brandy, anise extract, vanilla, and anise seeds in a small bowl to soften the seeds.

Beat sugar and butter with a mixer until it is fluffy, add eggs one at a time and blend well.

Measure flour and baking powder into separate bowl. Alternate adding flour mixture and brandy mixture to the creamed butter until all is incorporated into the dough and add almonds.

Form 4 logs (2 logs for larger biscotti) and place on cookie sheets using parchment paper.

Bake until golden brown, 30-40 minutes. Remove from oven and cool completely, reduce oven temp to 300*. Slice each log into 12-16 pieces and place on cookie sheet. Bake for additional 30 minutes, turning each biscotti every 10 minutes.

Bread Pudding

Recipe by Virginia Madden.

The night before the BBQ was, as John would call it, "A great hang." We would sit around while the brisket and pork shoulder were smoking and the pig was on the rotisserie. We'd crack open a couple bottles of wine. Myself and my friend George Leonard would make dinner for everyone, which was usually around 25 people. We'd usually make a pasta, fry some fresh sardines, sausage, cook up some wild game. Virginia always made her awesome bread pudding for the cooking crew for this night.

For the bread pudding:
1 loaf of old bread, sourdough works nicely, cut it into 1-inch pieces.
1 quart of milk
3 eggs
1 ½ cups sugar
1 tsp. vanilla
1 cup raisins, or any dried fruit of your preference
1 cup nuts, slivered almonds or walnut pieces work nicely

For the glaze:
1 stick butter
2 cups powdered sugar
2 eggs, beaten well
1 cup brandy, rum or whiskey

Preheat oven to 325°F.

Place bread in a baking dish, pour milk over it and let sit for an hour or overnight. Place in the fridge if you will be leaving it overnight.

In a mixing bowl, beat beat eggs well. Add sugar and continue to beat by hand until well incorporated. Add vanilla and mix in well.

Pour the egg mixture into the baking dish with the soaked bread and mix with a large spoon.

Sprinkle raisins and nuts over and bake for about an hour and 10 minutes, covered.

While bread pudding bakes, make the glaze. Melt butter in a double boiler. Once melted stir in powdered sugar and mix until smooth and creamy. Remove from heat and let cool slightly before mixing in eggs and alcohol.

Pour the glaze over the bread pudding and serve. Can be enjoyed hot or cold.

Lemon Cheesecake Bars

Recipe and photos by Kathryn Donangelo.

2 cups graham crackers
4 tbsp. unsalted butter, melted
2 (8 oz.) packages cream cheese
½ cup sugar
1 tsp. vanilla extract
2 tsp. fresh lemon zest
1-2 tbsp. fresh lemon juice, depending on how lemony you want the bars
2 large eggs

Preheat oven to 350°F.

Line an 8 x 8-inch baking dish with foil and grease with cooking spray.

In a food processor, pulse the graham crackers into crumbs. Add to a small bowl and mix in the melted butter with a fork until mixed well.

Pour the crumbs in the baking dish and press firmly into an even layer. I use the back of my measuring cup to make the layer and to make it extra firm.

With an electric mixer or stand mixer, beat together the cream cheese, sugar, vanilla extract, lemon zest, and juice until combined. Slowly add the eggs, one at a time, until each one is incorporated into the mixture. Use a spatula to scrape down the sides of the bowl and continue to mix until batter looks light and fluffy.

Add the mixture on top of the graham cracker crust and spread evenly.

Bake for 20-25 minutes, until the center is almost set.

Let the cheesecake cool completely and place in the refrigerator to set and get firm for at least 2 hours. Once set, cut with a sharp knife into bars. Enjoy with fresh berries, mint leaves or just plain.

Homemade Limoncello

Makes about three 750 mL bottles of limoncello

15 Meyer lemons, strips of rinds only, avoid any of the pith (the white part) if possible, freeze juice for later
2 750 mL bottles Everclear grain alcohol (150 proof)
5 cups of water
5 cups of sugar

Add one bottle of Everclear and lemon rinds in a big glass container, like one used for iced tea, etc. Make sure it's large enough to add the second bottle of Everclear and the simple syrup you will make.

Leave rinds in the Everclear for 40 days, and then add the other bottle of Everclear and 1 cup of the frozen lemon juice.

In a small saucepan, dissolve the sugar in the water to make a simple syrup, avoid boiling. Let cool and then add to the container.

After another 40 days, strain the rinds out. Store in freezer (it will not freeze) and enjoy!

INDEX

A
Almond Crusted Roasted Sea Bass, 98

B
Baccala Fritters, 108
Baked Pasta with Ricotta, 88
Balsamic Vinaigrette, 59
Basil Cream Sauce, 60
Beet Salad, 45
Biscotti, 145
Bracciolli (Stuffed Flank Steak), 120
Braised Red Cabbage, 13
Bread Pudding, 146
Breaded Squid, 104
Bruschetta, 17

C
Caesar Salad, 36
Cafe Fina Gazpacho Soup, 38
Cafe Fina Meatloaf, 114
Cannoli, 140
Caper Vinaigrette, 53
Cauliflower Mashed Potatoes, 11
Cioppino, 93
Classic Clams in Linguini, 66
Crabcakes, 14
Cream of Swiss Chard, 8
Creamy Italian Dressing, 59
Creole Mayonnaise, 56
Crostini, 29

D
David's Los Baños Lamb Stew, 46
Dipping Sauce for Strawberries, 137

F
Fettuccini Alfredo, 69
Fina's Finest BBQ Sauce, 52
Fresh BBQ'd Sardines, 10
Fresh Tomato Sauce, 51
Fried Squid Steaks, 105
Fresh Vegetable Soup, 34

G
Grilled Octopus, 27
Grilled Petrale Sole, 96

H
Homemade Limoncello, 151
How to Cook Artichokes, 6

I
Italian Ricotta Cookies, 135
Italian Sausage, 116
Italian Sausage & Spinach Egg Bites, 23
Italian Sausage Sandwich, 118
Italian-Style Roasted Peppers, 24

L
Lasagna with Sausage and Peas, 80
Lemon Butter Caper Sauce, 54
Lemon Cheesecake Bars, 148
Lentil Soup, 42
Loaded Sautéed Spinach, 4
Louie Dressing, 57

M
Marinara Sauce, 50
Mint Pesto, 54
Mom's Breaded Chicken, 126
Mom's Meatballs, 112
Mom's Minestrone Soup, 33
Mushroom Marsala Sauce, 53

N
No Mayo Cole Slaw, 37

O
Octopus Salad, 2
Orzo Pasta, 20

P
Pan-fried Sardines, 9
Pasta alla Vodka, 76
Pasta Bolognese, 75
Pasta Fina, 65
Pasta Gianna, 73
Pasta Puttanesca, 78
Pasta with Broccoli, 84
Pasta with Cauliflower, 83
Pasta with Eggplant, 85

Pasta with Peas, 82
Puff pastry shells with Veal (Veal *Vol-au-vent*), 127
Pistachio Pesto with Prawns over Penne, 71
Pizza Mia, 130
Pomegranate Marinated Lamb Chops, 124
Prosecco Mignonette Sauce for Oysters, 58

R

Rack of Lamb Dijon, 123
Rice with Squid, 107
Ricotta Cheesecake, 138
Roasted Chicken with Potatoes, Carrots, and Celery, 119
Roasted Garlic, 12
Roasted Wild Duck, 125
Rock Cod, 101
Rustic Olive Bread, 21

S

Salmon Burger, 100
Salmon Pasta, 77
Salmoriglio Sauce, 56
Sanddabs, 102
Sautéed Mussels, 19
Sautéed Swordfish with Eggplant and Mint over Fettuccini, 74
Seasoned Butter, 57
Seasoned Italian Cracker Meal, 29
Seasoned Italian Breadcrumbs, 29
Secret Sauce, 55
Sesame Cookies or Queen's Biscuits (*Biscottii di Regina*), 144
Shrimp Burger, 99
Sicilian BBQ Chicken, 115
Spiedini alla Siciliana, Grilled Beef Rolls, 128
Split Pea Soup, 35
Squid and Peas over Fussili, 86
Squid Balls, 106
Squid Cioppino, 94
Squid Salad, 41
Steamed Clams, 16
Stuffed Calamari, 95
Stuffed Veal Rollatini, 122

T

Tartar Sauce, 55

U

Ultimate Chocolate Cake, 142

W

Whole Roasted Cauliflower, 5